Winter's Tales

NEW SERIES: 4

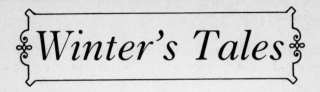

Winter's Tales

NEW SERIES: 4

*

EDITED BY

Robin Baird-Smith

St. Martin's Press

New York

Winter's tales (New York, N.Y. : 1985)
  Winter's tales. – New ser, 1- – New York: St. Martin's Press, c1985-
  v. ; 22 cm..
  Annual.
  Continues. Christmas feast.

  1. Short Stories – Periodicals.
PN6120.2.W56   808.83'1–dc19   86–655581
                         AACR 2   MARC-S

Library of Congress   [8703]

ISBN 0–312–02480–0

First U.S. Edition
10 9 8 7 6 5 4 3 2 1

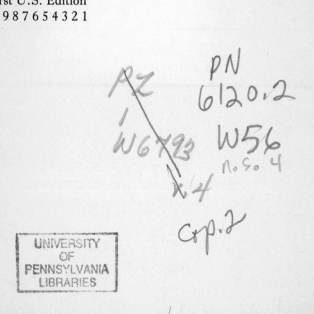

CONTENTS

[5]

ACKNOWLEDGEMENTS

The stories are copyright respectively:
© 1988 Francis King
© 1988 Norman Thomas di Giovanni and Susan Ashe
© 1988 David Leavitt
© 1988 Jeanette Winterson
© 1988 Damon Galgut
© 1988 Lawrence Scott
© 1988 Monica Furlong
© 1988 Peter Benson
© 1988 Sue Krisman
© 1988 Desmond Hogan
© 1988 Laura Kalpakian
© 1988 Helen Harris
© 1988 Robert Edric
© 1988 Norman Thomas di Giovanni and Susan Ashe

EDITOR'S NOTE

'The short story', wrote John Bayley, 'has a special technique for revealing a reality about life over and above the one it purports to show.' For well over thirty years, *Winter's Tales* has been its champion, even during the years when short stories were singularly out of fashion. But at long last it has once again found its strength as a literary form.

The stories in *Winter's Tales* are not commissioned with a particular theme in mind; they always show a variety of mood, style and length. This year, Augusto Monterroso has provided a gem of a few hundred words; Laura Kalpakian has contributed a very long short story. But for once many of the stories do seem to touch on a specific theme – mortality. Specifically the stories of Francis King, Robert Edric and Laura Kalpakian all concern elderly ladies with diminishing powers. At the other extreme Damon Galgut's story is about an intense relationship between two young men, with intimations of mortality perfectly evident to read.

This year the average age of the contributors is younger, I believe, than it has ever been before. This must be a good sign because one of the main purposes of *Winter's Tales* is to encourage new young writers. All the stories appear here in print for the first time with the exception of Jeanette Winterson's story 'Orion', which was first published in *Granta*. Any collection of stories containing the best of new young talent would have to include her. Her extraordinary novel *The Passion* has made a considerable impact and rightly so. It is pleasing too to be able to include a story by Francis King. He has contributed to *Winter's Tales* a number of times in the past and therefore represents the tradition. His story 'The Tradesman' shows him at his best.

Many reviewers last year remarked upon the absence of biographical notes. So for the first time in *Winter's Tales* these are included this year, rather reluctantly. I subscribe to J. M. W. Turner's view that 'the desire for biographical information about artists is both perfectly unsurprising and at the same time endearingly undiminished by our awareness of how little it helps us to understand or enjoy their art'.

What counts is the quality of the stories and this the reader must judge.

Robin Baird-Smith, 1988

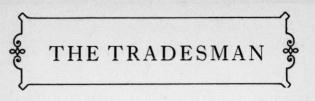

THE TRADESMAN

Francis King

An energy as vibrant and forceful as the screw of a liner propelled her through that day. The weeks of inertia, propped up in bed, slouched in the arm-chair or reclining on the sofa, the television only half-watched or the book or newspaper only half-read, might never have been. She had so often said, 'I no longer seem able to take anything in,' and now, as she hobbled on the zimmer from room to room, she could take in everything with a speed that both delighted and frightened her.

She wrote the letters which she had for so long been merely writing in her head. She went through the drawers of her kneehole desk and her old-fashioned, crocodile-leather writing-case, a twenty-first birthday present from her father long before the War, and tore up other letters, bills long since receipted, and ancient brochures from that far-off time when she had been well enough to travel and her beloved Harry had still been alive. She sorted out clothes, cheque-book stubs and even, in the kitchen – breathing heavily as, propped against the dresser, she strained to reach upwards – old packets of Smash, Bisto and Bird's Custard. Miraculously, she felt none of the usual giddiness, dull aching of the limbs, or that sensation of sweat pricking through the skin of her forehead like needles of ice.

The telephone rang. It was Ida, spinster friend of her spinster niece, Julia. 'Oh, Mrs Masterman, I didn't want to drag you to the phone. That was the last thing I wanted. But I promised Julia to give a call to see that all was well with you.'

'Yes, dear.'

'*Are* you all right?'

'Yes, I'm fine, Ida.'

In her tense, secretive way, Ida resented the amount of time that her best and almost only friend had to spend on this aunt. Such a disagreeable, demanding old woman, and so obstinate in her refusal to go into that home in Torquay which she and Julia had spent a whole broiling summer's day finding for her, Ida's feet swelling in a new pair of shoes and Julia complaining that the glare off the sea had given her a migraine.

'I'd like to come by to see you,' Ida lied. 'But we're so busy with our annual stocktaking all through this week. And this evening I must pop over to the hospital to see how Julia's getting on. Perhaps tomorrow evening . . .'

'No, dear, it's sweet of you to offer, but there'll be no need for that.'

Ungracious old slug! 'Oh, I'd be happy to come if I can manage it. It just depends on what time I get off.'

'There'll be no need, Ida. Really.'

'At all events it's good news that Julia came through the op so well. And nothing sinister found . . .'

'Yes, that was good news.'

Soon after that chubby, cheery Mrs Gore, a navy-blue headscarf tied low across her forehead so that she looked like an overgrown child disguised as a pirate for a fancy-dress party, was ringing at the door.

'Well, you opened up very quickly today! That shows you must be better.' Mrs Gore had a way of waddling from side to side, as though on a deck in a rough sea, as she transported the food into the sitting-room. She looked around her. 'Julia seems to have had a regular tidy-up in here, I see.' Mrs Gore must have forgotten that for the past three days Julia had been in hospital. Mrs Masterman did not reveal to her that it was she who had done the tidying.

'Toad-in-the-hole,' Mrs Gore announced enthusiastically. 'I know that's one of your favourites.'

Mrs Masterman, who liked Mrs Gore but disliked toad-in-the-hole, did not correct her. 'You're a great reader,' she said.

Mrs Gore, who had been English mistress at a girls' school before her marriage, said: 'Well, yes, I do read a lot. Much more than I ever watch the telly. That's a bone of contention between Jack and me – the telly, I mean.'

'Well, I put aside this edition of Joseph Conrad for you. A little present. You've always been so kind to me. It belonged to my late husband.' ('My late husband' – that was how Mrs Masterman always referred to him).

'Oh, but I couldn't accept such a beautiful edition. Really, Mrs Masterman. Honestly. It must be a – an heirloom.'

'I can only manage large print now.'

'But oughtn't Julia to have it? Or at least someone far more deserving than myself?'

'Julia's not a reader, I'm afraid. Or, at any rate, not a reader of Conrad,' Mrs Masterman added drily. 'And there's no one more deserving than you.'

Mrs Gore's plump cheeks flushed. She shook herself like a dog after someone has patted it, her rump swaying from side to side. Head tilted, she asked: 'Do you really want me to have them?'

'Of course. Otherwise I shouldn't have offered them to you.'

Mrs Gore often told her husband that she liked Mrs Masterman's 'straightness'. She liked it now.

'Well, in that case . . .'

Mrs Gore began to gather up the books. 'You'd better

[13]

start on that –' her head indicated the toad-in-the-hole – 'before it gets cold.'

But Mrs Masterman never started on the toad-in-the-hole. Although usually she looked forward so eagerly through the long, empty day for the arrival of Mrs Gore in her little Meals-on-Wheels van, the colour of an over-ripe cherry, today she had no appetite. When, as a child, her parents would order her to eat, she would complain: 'But I don't feel hungry! Today's a special day.' Today was once more a special day.

She wondered whether to attempt to mount the stairs. But it was years since she had managed to do that, so that upstairs had long since become Julia's kingdom, to which she and Ida would retreat ('You won't feel lonely, will you, auntie? It's just that Ida and I have some things to discuss in private') after they had done their duty (they often used that phrase) with the often gruff and grumpy old woman, who appeared to be so much deafer with them than with anyone else. There were things gathering dust in the little guest-room which was now never used, and even more things gathering dust in the attic. 'One day we really must have a turn-out,' Julia would say, after she had gone into one or the other. Well, one day she could have it.

Soon after four, little Molly arrived, so neat and so bright, with her shoulder-length hair glistening in the slanting October sunlight as Mrs Masterman opened the door to her. She too remarked on how quickly Mrs Masterman had arrived at the door. She held her bag before her, in both her small, plump hands, as she stepped across the threshold.

'Aren't you cold, my dear?'

'I never feel the cold. I walked all the way here, since the bus took so long in coming. I hope I'm not late.'

'Not so that it matters.' Mrs Masterman was always truthful.

'Why did you decide on a week instead of a fortnight this time?' Molly asked as she began to set out all the tools of her trade on the table in the bedroom. 'Are you expecting someone special?'

Mrs Masterman gave a small smile, without answering the question.

Molly crossed over to the basin and began running the water, fingers fluttering under it. 'It's coming hot more quickly than usual.'

'Is it?'

'Usually it takes quite a time.'

'That's such an old boiler. Should have been replaced years and years ago. But since it does its job – after a fashion . . .'

'It's probably not very economical . . .'

As she first washed and then set Mrs Masterman's hair, Molly chatted away, as she usually chatted away, about her boy-friend, who was in the army in Germany. He had been promised leave and then, for a variety of reasons, he had not received it.

'How disappointing for you!' Mrs Masterman sighed. 'You should get married and then you could be out there with him.'

'But the thing is – I'm not yet really *sure*.'

'Yes, one must be sure. That's always important.' She herself had been wholly sure. She was wholly sure now.

'What fine hair you've got! Like a baby's.'

At each of her visits Molly said that.

'Too fine. So difficult to keep in place.'

'And how's your niece?' Molly, who did not care for Julia – she spoke in such a hard, bossy way – always asked that too.

'Well, she's in hospital. A little operation. Just one of these women's things. Nothing serious.'

'Oh, I'm glad – that it's not serious, I mean!' Molly, who often blushed, blushed now.

When Molly had finished and was carefully putting all her things back into the bag, Mrs Masterman said: 'Oh, Molly, I have a little present for you. I was tidying up my drawers and I came on it. It's over there, on the dressing-table. The cameo brooch. On the little china tray.'

Molly was astounded. She also felt uneasy. She went over to the dressing-table and put out a hand and touched the brooch, without picking it up. It was carved with the head of a woman. 'Oh, but Mrs Masterman . . . I *couldn't*!'

'It belonged to my mother and to her mother before that. It's early Victorian. Nothing special,' she added quickly, afraid that its antiquity might make Molly even more reluctant to take it. 'You've always been so kind to me, I've always so much enjoyed our meetings.' Then, seeing that Molly was still hesitating, she said: 'Take it, dear! Unless, of course, you don't like it. Unless you feel it's something you'd never wear.'

'Oh, I *love* it! It's – it's ever so elegant!'

'Then take it, take it!'

'But wouldn't your niece . . .?'

'Oh, she has a lot of jewellery – her mother's, mine. And she never wears it. She doesn't care for jewellery. Not as I used to do at her age.'

Molly at last picked up the brooch, with a strange mingling of pleasure, foreboding and guilt. 'I'll wear it now.' She pinned it to her pink blouse, high up, almost under her small, pointed chin.

'Lovely!' Mrs Masterman exclaimed. 'It suits you. Just right.'

[16]

Molly looked at herself in the dressing-table mirror. 'Just right.' She nodded. Her fingers rested on the cameo, feeling now its smoothness and now its roughness.

When Molly moved away from the dressing-table, Mrs Masterman then looked at her own reflection. 'Oh, Molly, you've excelled yourself!'

'Well, it seemed to go exactly right today. Don't ask me why! I've noticed that. Sometimes, however hard I try, it doesn't go right, not really right. And then one day . . . I've never seen it look nicer.'

'I wanted it to look nice.'

Who could the old pet be expecting? Some boy-friend from the past? Or just the doctor or her solicitor? Molly wanted to ask but did not dare to do so. If Mrs Masterman wanted her to know, she would tell her. If she didn't want her to know, she would merely smile and ignore any direct questioning or indirect probing, as she so often did.

'Dear Molly!'

Mrs Masterman put up her hands from the chair and, as she did so, Molly found herself lowering her head, the golden hair falling forwards. The hands rested one on either of her cheeks. Then the lips, unexpectedly warm, moist and soft, touched Molly's mouth for a brief moment. The old woman had never kissed her before, but it seemed perfectly natural and in no way surprising that now she should do so.

'I'll show myself out . . . Oh, the cameo is lovely! Thank you, thank you! Bob will never believe that *you* gave it to me. He'll think some other boy gave it to me and he'll be terribly, terribly jealous!' She laughed. She liked the idea of his being jealous of old Mrs Masterman.

When Molly had gone, Mrs Masterman sat on for a

[17]

while in the bedroom, gazing at her reflection in the mirror. Yes, her hair, silvery and thin, had never looked better. The hair of a baby, the hair of a very old woman. She stroked it gently and briefly with the palm of a hand. Then she hauled herself out of the chair and made her way into the sitting-room. She looked at the watch which she wore pinned to her cardigan, peering down to do so. Nearly five. Well, he'd be here soon.

But five passed and then quarter-past five and still he didn't come. These days one could never rely on anyone to come on time to do anything for one. Last week it had been the gasman to repair the heater in her bedroom. Each day she had telephoned and each day she had been told that, yes, he would be with her that morning or that afternoon. Finally, when he had turned up, he had told her that the fire needed some new radiants, which he had omitted to bring with him. The week before that, it had been the man to measure the sofa in Julia's 'den' (the word that she herself used for the little upstairs sitting-room to which she and Ida would retire) for some loose covers. 'One hears so much about unemployment,' Julia had grumbled, 'but when one *does* have a job to be done, there's no one in the least interested in doing it.'

At half-past five, Mrs Masterman went to the window and, propping herself against the wall beside it, gazed out into the already darkening street. Two of the children, a boy and a girl, who belonged to the Irish family next door – Julia was constantly complaining about their noise or the squalor of the garden from which that noise so often emanated – raced along the pavement, their faces screwed up with effort. No doubt they were afraid of missing something on their television. Mrs Masterman could often hear that television through the

[18]

wall, as she could often hear the father and mother shouting at each other.

A car passed and then another. She thought that the first, a battered Peugeot, might be his. That swish white Mercedes couldn't be. Oh, it was too bad! Perhaps he was not going to come after all today. And she'd gone to so much trouble to prepare everything.

The light of the bicycle, faint and wavering from side to side in the dusk, was the first thing that she saw. Then she saw the bicycle itself, an old-fashioned one with high handlebars, and then she saw the figure sitting erectly stiff on it. He did not look as she had expected him to look and yet she knew at once that, yes, this was he. He was wearing a rubber cape and a cap pulled down low over his forehead and – she screwed up her eyes – brown boots, highly laced, not shoes. All at once she was reminded of the man who used to come each week, on a bicycle not unlike this one and in a similar rubber cape, similar cap and similar boots, to wind the clocks of her grandfather's house in Norfolk. That man and her present visitor shared the same benignly gnome-like appearance.

She had opened the door before he had had time to ring the bell.

'Is it all right if I leave my bike here – behind these bushes? Don't want anyone to see it.'

'Yes, of course.'

'Lucky no one saw me approaching.'

At that he scuttled into the house. Once in, he pulled off his cap to reveal that it had left a mark, red and raw-looking, across his forehead. His hair fell long and greasy over his pointed ears, but the baldness at the back of his skull suggested a tonsure. Next he removed the rubber cape, with a swishing, sucking sound, and placed it, over the cap, on the hall chair.

[19]

'Sorry to be late,' he said, rubbing together hands mauve with cold. 'But the last job took longer than I'd expected.'

'It doesn't matter. You look cold,' she added.

'Should have brought some gloves. But early this afternoon . . . An Indian summer.'

They went into the sitting-room, she hobbling ahead of him on the zimmer. Once in, he hurried over to the windows and pulled the curtains across. 'You should have pulled the curtains. Hope no one saw me.'

'Yes. Yes, I'm sorry . . . Can I offer you anything before – before we begin?'

'No. Thank you. Nothing. As a matter of fact, I never drink tea or coffee or, indeed, any alcoholic beverages. My body doesn't need that kind of stimulus. In fact, it rebels against it.' On the telephone, she had thought his way of speaking old-fashioned. She thought so even more now. Yes, he was uncannily like that man who used to come to wind the clock and about whom there was some mystery, dark, sad and perhaps even disreputable, never to be revealed to her.

'You'll want some water.'

'Yes, I have it. Here.' She pointed to the carafe set out, a glass beside it, on a lace doiley, worked by her mother, on a silver tray which she herself had polished at the start of that long day.

'Fine. You'd be amazed how many people expect *me* to do everything. I can see that you're an independent spirit.'

She liked that. 'Yes, I've always been an independent spirit. All my life.'

He felt in a pocket of his loose-fitting cardigan and drew out a beige envelope.

'They're in there?' she said.

[20]

'That's right. Now you make yourself comfy, there's a good girl. Lie down on the sofa, put your legs up.'

'No. I'll sit here. That's how I planned it.' She placed herself in the armchair by the window, settling her head back on the pillow in its white linen cover fringed with lace.

'That's fine,' he said. 'If that's how you want it.'

'That's how I want it.'

He was about to pour some of the pills out of the envelope into his own cupped palm, but she stopped him. 'Give them to me here.' She held out a hand.

He tipped the pills into her palm. Then he went over to the carafe and poured water out from it into the tumbler.

'I've always been bad at swallowing pills.' She smiled up at him placatingly, as in recent years she had so often smiled up at nurses and doctors.

'Take your time.'

She swallowed three of the pills, one after the other. It was far easier than she had ever supposed. She pointed. 'Later – I want you to use that ribbon over there. You won't forget, will you?'

'I'll make everything as nice as possible. Don't you worry.' He picked up the pale blue ribbon and began to wrap it round his right forefinger. The finger was long and bony, the nail had a ridge of dirt under it.

'Your – your envelope is on the mantelpiece.'

'Oh, don't worry about that, dear! Don't worry about anything!'

She smiled. 'You're very efficient, I must say.' Nowadays one didn't expect people to be efficient when they came to do things for one.

'Go on swallowing those pills.'

She went on swallowing them. Eventually, her breath became shallow, there was a blue tinge to her lips

[21]

and her eyelids. The eyelids fluttered, fluttered again, closed. From a pocket of the cardigan he drew out a transparent plastic bag. Gently, kneeling now beside her, he placed it over her head. He took the length of ribbon and stretched it taut between one hand and the other. Then he circled it loosely around her throat and tied it in a bow.

Through the bag, he saw her lips moving. She was saying something or trying to say something. What, what? Then he realized. She was saying 'Thank you, thank you, thank you.'

SHORT STORY CONTEST

Marcos Aguinis

Translated from the Spanish by
Norman Thomas di Giovanni and Susan Ashe

Eduardo flung his coat at the sofa, let out a weary sigh, and said he was going to tell me an amazing story. His face wore a grim look, yet at the same time he radiated a distinct glow. When I offered to get him some coffee, he put an imperious halt to it.

'Later,' he said. 'Right now sit down and listen.'

He unbuttoned his collar and sat back. Before he could get going, his hand waved away the words that were fighting to come out of his mouth. His eyes, which had grown small and bleary, told of the effort he was making to set his complicated tale in order. In the end, he opted for asking me whether I'd ever judged a short story contest.

I shrugged. Sure, several times. Why? Because, he said, momentarily carried away, what had happened to him had never happened before in any competition since the year dot. His mistake had been – maybe it was his vanity, maybe the money – to accept too readily and then to find himself smack in the midst of an uncontainable muddle. He wasn't exaggerating, he said, just airing his chagrin. And his partial joy.

I couldn't follow him, but neither could I hide my curiosity.

Eduardo is an obsessive writer who has achieved a moderate success with his two novels and four story collections. He's manic about his style and, to his publisher's despair, pitiless about last-minute tinkering. Scouring his first book for its few typos – three, to be exact – so affected his eyesight that he was forced to visit three oculists in the space of a single month and then to swear an oath never to reread anything he wrote once it appeared in print.

Years back, he told me, he'd had to judge the offerings of a local group, but, as a contest, that had been a nonentity. When he'd been approached this time, what bowled him over was the huge sum of money he was offered as a fee. Although tempted, he feigned lack of interest, since the sponsor of the affair was a new supermarket whose public relations man thought he could exploit literature to draw customers.

I interrupted Eduardo to say one couldn't help seeing posters about the contest. Buenos Aires was plastered with them.

What he most disliked, Eduardo growled, was this coupling of supermarkets and creative writing, of literary genres and mass-produced foods, the debasement of fiction to make people buy sausages. He disliked it and, what was worse, he was stupid to dislike it, because these days literature itself was mass-produced, and short stories and novels were on sale in any supermarket.

No, it was he who was behind the times, he who was inconsistent. This became only too plain to Eduardo on the day he met the PR man to sign their agreement. While trying to put on the air of a connoisseur of the arts, the man came out with one or two clangers that turned Eduardo's ears red. But the man also handed over a fat advance that delighted Eduardo, though at the same time it filled him with shame. Knowing he was in it only for the money, how could he then condemn the supermarket man for promoting this literary extravaganza only for the money?

In the next few weeks, before any of the stories were submitted, Eduardo had tried to put this surrender of his principles out of mind. Besides, who was going to write a story on a topic as inane as the one stipulated by the PR man – The Supermarket in Today's World? This genius' one concern was retailing, and it didn't matter to him one dried fig or one tiny tin of peas that anyone might possibly want to write about something else. He was sure there'd be a flood of entries. However, in the event that there wasn't, the important thing was that the competition should make an impact. The company would guarantee a winner, and under no circumstances would the contest be declared null and void. After all, the PR man was not going to forgo the trappings of the presentation ceremony, when he himself would confer the diploma, the medal, and the resounding check.

The vehemence with which Eduardo recounted the affair amused me. It was a short story in itself and maybe the best one that would come out of the contest – a story of stories, or metastory, as those who specialize in eviscerating literature might say.

While he waited for the manuscripts to arrive on his doorstep, Eduardo found growing in him an abhorrence of assembly-line techniques, which insidiously force to the wall all craftsmen, among whom he numbered the writer; an abhorrence of PR men, whose diabolical mission it is to corrupt natural relationships for the purpose of making money; an abhorrence of contests, which hold out the promise of reward for merit and end by breaking the promise and making a nonsense of merit; an abhorrence of bad writing, which he was soon to be gorging on; an abhorrence of himself for condoning the theme of the contest; an abhorrence, in short, of the whole damned thing. I could imagine Eduardo sticking his fingers down his throat to make himself spew up all his most deep-seated aversions.

Two months passed, and Eduardo had spent the best part of the advance. Then, one day, there arrived a cardboard box emblazoned with the shining emblem of the contest and containing twenty-eight stories together with a short and sweet letter from the PR man. Eduardo was astounded. He had not expected so many entries; surely, it had to be a load of junk. What else could anyone write about supermarkets?

Flipping through the folders, he read some of the titles. 'Honey and Waffles', 'A Colorful Saunter', 'The Joy of Shopping Carts', 'The Diet of a Superstore Buff'. Eduardo's first reaction had been to shut the box and hold it shut tight for several minutes to prevent its noxious contents from getting out and polluting the air. Then he tore the letter up into small pieces and threw them one by one into the wastepaper basket.

The first unfortunate upshot was that for several days he couldn't write a word. Or read. Instead, he racked his brain for ways to break the contract, though by now he could not pay back the advance. In this strait-jacket and unable to think clearly, Eduardo refused to swallow the folderfuls of tripe. Such lethal outpourings of unmitigated hogwash, he feared, might damage his brain cells.

His wife Irene tried to reason with him, but to no avail. After a week or so, he once more dared open the box, which he'd hidden in the farthest and darkest corner of his study, hoping the mildew would make inroads on it. This time he spotted other improbable titles, such as 'Jesus Goes Shopping', 'The Extraterrestrial Supermarket', 'Adventures of a Tinned Man', and 'Supermarket Baby'.

Shutting his eyes, Eduardo picked out a story at random – 'The Victory of Samothrace'. A title with classical associations, a reference to antiquity, a certain respect for the arts. Perhaps this one was palatable.

'What an old fool you are, Eduardo!' Eduardo shouted at himself. What had the Winged Victory to do with a supermarket? Or, put another way, how clever the writer must have been to link the two. Eduardo was assailed by conflicting ideas. Had he been too reactionary before this and was he now falling over himself to compensate for it by feeling sudden sympathy for the contest? Tales inspired by shabby street markets were legitimate enough. Why not give expression to the experiences and daydreams inspired in people today by ample shopping carts, fancy packaging, well-trained checkout girls, and the mingled aromas of both homely and exotic products?

Eduardo scanned a few more titles: 'The Supermarket Inferno', 'A Grocer's Guide to the Galaxy', 'Love Among the Chocolates', 'The Kinky Checkout Girl', 'The White Wine Murders'. This was more like it, he thought. A touch ingenuous, perhaps, but not bad. Who could tell, it might even prove to be the style of our times. The new was always irritating and disagreeable at first – but only at first. Since signing the contract, some of Eduardo's cherished beliefs were showing cracks. He could accept that contemporary writing might be evolving in the direction of a supermarket genre, but was he cut out to write it?

His spirits sank when, to his surprise, he received a second box, containing a further thirty-six stories. Even Irene felt dismay, and she had to make a fresh effort to find words to soothe him. Hadn't the first twenty-eight stories been the total number of entries? Hadn't the submission date closed? Apparently not. Another sixty-five boxes arrived at Eduardo's house, each with about thirty folders, making a grand total of nearly two thousand short stories.

It's an outrage! A scandal! A swindle! groaned Eduardo. It's a colossal success! rejoiced the PR man in his latest note, short and sweet as ever.

Titles began swarming in Eduardo's head: 'The Terrorist Lollipop', 'Sex and the Delivery Boy', 'The Egg Smugglers', 'Yoghurts of Death'. He gargled insults and spat them out like grapeshot at the supermarket's PR man, who was the most despicable, cynical, parasitic creature under the sun and who had not only snared Eduardo with money but was out to make him work like a slave, to the last drop of sweat, for the fees that had once seemed so generous. Just the thought of the mountain of dross his brain would have to absorb pressed on Eduardo like a weight.

While Eduardo read, Irene did her best to keep the boxes and folders in order. Like unwanted guests, they seemed to be constantly shifting about from place to place, monopolizing chairs and beds and driving their timid hosts into corners. Irene was relentless in keeping a few passageways free, but she was unable to dislodge the piles of folders from bedroom, bathroom, living-room, or kitchen.

At the beginning and end of each tale he read, Eduardo grumbled that he would never be able to read two thousand stories. Still, he forged ahead. 'The Jewel in the Beetroot' he found ingenious and quite well written; 'Store-room Romance' gave him a chuckle; and 'Saccharine in the Carry-cot' he thought poignant. But the rest were mostly dreary, cliché-ridden, and fit only for stoking the boiler.

Within a day or two, Irene stopped nagging him about doing the job properly, and Eduardo took to reading far into the night. His earlier derision now turned to addiction. Exhausting page after page, his eyes grew bloodshot from words and metaphors, baked beans and derring-do, caloried seductions and futuristic settings, pedestrian language and the occasional high-flown phrase. He looked for genuine creativity but settled for mediocrity and ineptitude so long as a work was even remotely original in its portrayal of human conflict. One story in twenty-five or thirty was.

A handful of tales verged on science fiction, and in one the supermarket's drug section offered for sale ampules of dehydrated semen with which women could perform do-it-yourself insemination in the comfort of their homes. The back of the package listed the baby's genetic traits, and the product came with a choice of applicator: the plain economy model or the electron-ically-controlled, easy-to-operate inflatable doll with a selection of nineteen different styles of love-making.

Another story along similar lines dealt with a game from the toy section. Its object was to select sets of chromosomes from a glossy leaflet and combine them to construct beasts from the mythologies of ancient Egypt, Greece, and India. A more expensive and ambitious version of this game, designed for several competitors, involved a computer to concoct new monsters. Soon terri-fying beasts emitting hideous sounds were proliferating in children's rooms, running amok and threatening a blood-bath. In the end, a leviathan's scale short-circuits the computer, painlessly vaporizing a child's arm.

Irene had advised him to read the first few lines of each story, to proceed obliquely through the subse-quent pages, and not linger unless the piece were any good. Surely this was the way all contests were judged the world over. By then, Eduardo had found it imposs-ible even to read this small amount. But after 'The Absentminded Stock-taker', 'The Erotic Depilatory',

[31]

and 'Takeaway Mythology' something changed. Now he became as meticulous in his reading as he had hitherto been in his writing.

Just as he got through half the folders, the PR man telephoned to remind Eduardo that he was to come to the office in three days' time to confirm the winning entry. As a prestigious writer and as a member of the prestigious panel of judges, Eduardo was, after all, a living symbol of Argentine literature.

Eduardo felt an attack of palpitations coming on. There was no way he could finish the hundreds of remaining stories. He babbled a plea for an extension.

Impossible, replied the PR man, because the ceremony at which the fabulous prize was to be presented had already been announced. He went on to cite the television channels that would be providing coverage and the guest stars who would be in attendance, and he assured Eduardo that to a gifted writer like himself three days were more than adequate in which to spot the talent from among the thousand stories Eduardo still had not got around to reading.

In three days, then, a van would come from the supermarket to collect all the stories, which, as a further gesture of the company's meticulousness, efficiency, and courtesy, would promptly be returned to their authors. Eduardo felt more panic-stricken than ever.

Irene massaged the back of his neck. In three days he'd also get the rest of his money, which was the reason he had got involved in the first place. But Eduardo didn't mind having the money later if only he could finish reading the stories. His wife found this incomprehensible. The contest had upset their daily routine, their love-life, their married bliss, and now here was Irene having to call a doctor, for suddenly Eduardo was struck down by a violent bout of diarrhoea.

[32]

Sedatives were powerless to relieve his galloping anxiety, and during the doctor's examination Eduardo could not tear his eyes from the nearest folder. Throwing up his hands in despair, the doctor told the patient he must choose between his health and an absurd sense of fair play. Eduardo said he no longer cared about fairness or about who won. What interested him was rescuing those few good stories dotted like nuggets of gold among the bad ones. The doctor, however much he scratched his head, was at a loss to fathom Eduardo's passion.

It was a passion that went unrewarded. The van arrived on time. Two men and three women burst into the apartment and set about searching every nook and cranny as if engaged on a police raid. So Eduardo felt it; so Irene wanted it. Every last folder was collected, even those hidden in drawers, under the sofa, and between books. Doubled up with diarrhoea, Eduardo forced open one or two boxes and tried to slip a few folders under the carpet. But the round-up was both thorough and relentless, and every last nugget was spirited away. Now storyless, Eduardo swallowed more pills, but to no avail.

He shaved, put a roll of toilet paper in his briefcase, and set off for the supermarket. The PR man welcomed him with a big public-relations smile. He sat Eduardo at his desk and surrounded him with three secretaries, or bodyguards, or hired actors. Which, Eduardo couldn't tell. The three kept shoving papers under his nose – the endless list of entries, a copy of the contract Eduardo had signed months before, the diploma for first prize with the winner's name already on it and underneath the signatures of the PR man and a local dignitary. All that was missing was Eduardo's signature.

The contest had been a tremendous success. It was already the talk of the neighborhood, and after the

[33]

ceremony would be the talk of all Buenos Aires. Eduardo balked. He hadn't been able to read all the material. To which the PR man replied that it was superfluous to go over all that again, since the conversation in which Eduardo had asked for an extension had been duly taped. The request was in serious breach of the clause in the contract committing Eduardo to finish his reading within two months. Of course, the supermarket was more than willing to overlook this point, nor would it ask for its money back.

Brandishing a checkbook, the PR man waited for Eduardo to put his signature to the diploma. Then the check could be written and the tape destroyed. After that, the man said, he would shake Eduardo's hand and invite him to enjoy the grand ceremony, where before his very eyes he would behold the massive boost in his prestige as a writer. There was no question of Eduardo's playing the ivory-tower purist and refusing to award the prize to the supermarket's choice just because he hadn't read half the manuscripts. After all, the PR man's tender smile seemed to say as he held out the check, you went into this job like a whore and came out of it falling in love.

'Now then,' Eduardo finished, 'how about that coffee of yours? I think I could use it.'

SPOUSE NIGHT

David Leavitt

During the day, when Arthur is at work, the puppy listens to the radio – 'anything with voices,' Mrs Theodorus advised when Arthur went to pick up the puppy; 'it calms them.' And so, sitting in her pen in Arthur's decaying kitchen, while she chews on the newspaper which is meant to be her toilet, or urinates on the towel which is meant to be her bed, the puppy is surrounded by a comforting haze of half-human noise. For a while Arthur tried WQRT, the leftist station, and the puppy heard interviews with experts on Central American insurgency and radical women of color. Then he tuned into a station which broadcast exclusively for the Polish community. 'Mrs Byziewicz, who has requested this polka, is eighty-five, the mother of three and the grand-mother of eleven,' the puppy heard as she pounced on her rubber Snoopy newspaper, or tried to scale the chicken-wire walls of her pen. Now Arthur's settled on WSXT, a peculiar station which claims to feature "lite" programming, and which Arthur thinks is ideally suited to the listening needs of a dog, so the puppy is hearing, for the fourth time, a ten-minute-long radio play about Edgar Allan Poe, when Arthur rushes in the door with Mrs Theodorus, both breathing hard. 'Edgar, why are your poems so strange and weird?' Mrs Poe is asking her husband on the radio, and the puppy looks at the woman who midwifed her birth ten weeks earlier. Mrs Theodorus' blouse is partially undone, and the draw-string on her purple sweatpants is loosened, but all the puppy notices is the faint, half-familiar smell of her

[37]

mother, and smelling it, she cries, barks and, for the first time in her short life, leaps over the edge of her pen. No one is there to congratulate her. Sniffing, the puppy makes her way into the bedroom, where Arthur and Mrs Theodorus are in the midst of a sweaty half-naked tumble. The puppy jumps into the fray, barking, and Mrs Theodorus screams.

'Arthur, you have got to teach her who's boss,' she says, and climbs off of him. 'Remember – you must be in control at all times.' She looks down at the puppy, who sits on the ground now, humbled before the sight of Mrs Theodorus, naked except for her black bra, disapproval shining in her eyes. A small trickle of moisture snakes through the thick-pile carpet, darkening its yellow whorls, and quickly, quicker than Arthur can believe, Mrs Theodorus has the puppy in hand and is carrying her back into the kitchen, shouting, 'No! No!' She returns with a sponge and a bottle of urine stain remover. 'I'm a whiz at this,' she says.

'Eva,' Arthur says, rolling over and unbuttoning his pants, 'you never fail to amaze me.'

Across the house the puppy wails for her mother.

In Arthur's bathroom one medicine cabinet is full, one empty, but still, for some reason, on the soap dish, one of Claire's earrings hangs haphazardly, as if she'd just pulled it out of the tiny hole in her earlobe. Next to it lies a fake gold tooth, from the days when crowns were removeable, which Claire wore most of her life and only took out during her last stay in the hospital. Arthur saved the earring because he couldn't find its partner; for hours he searched the bedroom and the bathroom, desperate to complete his inventory of Claire's jewelry so that he could finally get rid of it all, but the second earring failed to materialize. Finally he gave up. After the rest of the jewelry was distributed among the children and Claire's sisters he could not bring himself to throw the one earring away – it would have killed him, he said in group. It is a gold earring, shaped like a dolphin; its tiny jade eye glints up at him from the syrupy moat of the soap dish.

'Have you been brushing her regularly?' Mrs Theodorus asks, examining the puppy on the kitchen table. 'Her furnishings look a little matted. Remember, Arthur, this is a high-maintenance dog you've got here, and you'd better get in the habit of taking care of her now if you don't want her to scream when she goes to the groomer later on.'

'I'm sorry, Eva,' Arthur says.

Mrs Theodorus smiles. 'Well, I'll be happy to help you,' she says, as yelping loudly, the puppy tries to bite the comb which is pulling the fur from her skin. 'But you've got to remember,' Mrs Theodorus adds, looking at Arthur sternly, 'she's your puppy, and finally it's your responsibility to take care of her. You can't count on me being around all the time to do it.'

'We're going to be late, Eva,' Arthur says.

'I know. I'll be done in a minute.'

She finishes, and the puppy is returned to the dark, private world in which she spends most of her time. 'What I'm interested in, Kathy,' a voice on the radio says, 'is how *you* feel when your husband makes these suggestions. You have to think about your own desires too.'

'That puppy is going to be ruined, listening to Dr Pleasure,' Mrs Theodorus says as she gets into her car. They still go in separate cars.

It is the third Thursday of the month – spouse night –

[39]

and even though Arthur and Mrs Theodorus are no longer technically spouses – both have recently lost their loved ones – they still attend with needful regularity. Claire, Arthur's wife, died two months ago of a sudden, searing chemical burn, a drug reaction, which over five days crisped and opened her skin until she lay in the burn unit, her face tomato-red, her body wrapped in mummy-like bandages, and wrote to Arthur, her hand shaking, 'I'm scared.' 'Scared of what?' Arthur asked, and she pointed a bloody finger, as best she could, to the tubes thrust down her throat to keep her breathing; she had pneumonia. In the terrible humidity of the burn-unit, surrounded by the screams of injured children, Arthur tried to reassure her. He had on three gowns, two masks, a flowered surgical cap, rubber gloves. His spectacled eyes stared out from all that fabric. A children's tapedeck he had bought at Walgreen's played Edith Piaf songs in the corner. Above it the nurse had written: 'Hello, my name is Claire. Please turn over the tape in my tapedeck. Thanx.'

Meanwhile, Mr Theodorus – jolly, warm, wonderful Mr Theodorus, with his black suits, his little mustache, his slicked-back hair; Mr Theodorus, brother-of-the-maître-d' at The Greek Tycoon's, mixer of the best daquiris and joy of group night – was in a coma a few floors below. Arthur and Mrs Theodorus met, shaken, to drink coffee in the cafeteria with the tired-out residents. They shook their heads, and sometimes they wept, before returning to the ordeal, the vigil. Mrs Theodorus told Arthur that her champion bitch Alicia was dying as well, of canine degenerative myleopathy; when she wasn't with Spiro she was at the animal hospital, stroking Alicia and feeding her small pieces of boiled chicken through the slats in her cage. She talked often, while she drank her coffee, about Alicia's coat. It

was the best coat in the country, she said. Walking out
of the cafeteria, Mrs Theodorus said she honestly did
not know which was going to hurt worse: the death of
her husband or of her dog. They parted at the third
floor. Riding back to the burn unit Arthur rallied to face
his own terrible dilemma of which-was-worse: the
possibility that Claire had died without him versus the
probability that she was still alive.

Arthur and Mrs Theodorus now return to the hospital only once a month, for spouse night. Olivia, the
social worker, insists that they are welcome to continue
coming to group as long as they want. And Arthur does
want to come. He depends on the group not only for
continuity, but because towards the end it constituted
the very center of Claire's life; in some ways the
members were more important to her than he was, or
the children. Still, he is afraid of becoming like Mrs
Jaroslavsky, who attends spouse night faithfully even
now, a year after Mr Jaroslavsky's passing. Because of
Mrs Jaroslavsky, the big conference table is covered
each spouse night with a pink tablecloth and platters of
poppy-seed cake, chocolate cake, pudding cake, blue-
berry pie. Each month there is an excuse, because each
month brings dark news, death and sudden spasms of
hope in equal quantity. This week, Mrs Jaroslavsky
explains, the cakes are because Christa is having her
six-month interim x-rays, and she wants to help.
'Everyone does what they can,' she says to Christa.
'What I do, is cook.'

Across the room, Christa – freckled arms, a long
sandy braid and a spigot in her arm for the chemo-
therapy to be poured into – looks away from the food,
biting the thumbnail of one hand, while Chuck, her
husband, holds the other. They are both professional
ski teachers, but have been living in this snowless cli-

mate since the illness, hand-to-mouth; Kitty Mitsui got Chuck a job busing dishes at Beefsteak Hirosha's, but that hardly scratches the surface of the bills.

'Thank you, Mrs Jaroslavsky,' Chuck says now, smiling faintly, then turning again to make sure Christa isn't going to cry.

'Well, you're welcome,' Mrs Jaroslavsky says. 'You know I do what I can. And if you need anything else – anything cooked, anything cleaned – don't hesitate to ask.'

She sits back, satisfied, in her chair, and takes out her knitting. She is a large, amiable-looking woman with red cheeks and hair, and oddly, the odor that dominates the room tonight is not that of the food, but the faint, sickly-sweet, waxy perfume of her lips. Arthur and Mrs Theodorus, taking off their coats, know, as some do not, that underneath the pink cloth is a table stained with cigarette burns, and pale, slightly swollen lesions where coffee cups have leaked, and chicken-scratched nicks in the wood where hands have idly ground pencils or scissor points or the ends of ballpoint pens. The carpet is pale yellow and worn in places, and over the table is a poster, its corners worn through with pin-prickings, of a cat clinging to a chinning bar. 'We all have days like this,' the poster says.

It is a hard room for the healthy; it looks like death. But the members of the group don't seem to notice, much less mind it. When she came home from group those first few Thursday nights, in fact, her tires skidding the gravel, Arthur had sometimes asked Claire what the room was like, and she had said, 'Oh, you know. Just a room.' This was before Arthur stopped repressing and started going to spouse night. After taking off her coat, Claire went straight out onto the porch and smoked a cigarette, and Arthur stood by the kitchen window, watching her as she blew rings into the night. She stared at the sky, at the stars, and that was how Arthur knew the group was changing her life. She looked exhilarated, like a girl dropped off from a date in which a boy she could not care less about has told her that he loves her.

Arthur still cannot quite believe, looking at her this spouse night, that he and Mrs Theodorus have become lovers. It seems a most unlikely thing for them to be doing, not three months after their loved ones' deaths. Still, even now, staring at her across the room, he is filled with the panicked desire for Eva which has characterized this affair since it began. For the first time in his life Arthur feels lust, insatiable lust, and apparently Eva feels it too. They make love wildly, whispering obscene phrases in each other's ears, howling with pleasure. He has scratch marks on his back from Eva's long nails. Sometimes, in the middle of the night, they get up and sit in her kitchen and eat giant pieces of the chocolate cream pie and Black Forest cake which Mr Theodorus' brother sends over from his restaurant. The whipped cream dots their noses and chins. Once they spread it on each other and licked it off, which Arthur had read about people doing in *Penthouse*; it was Eva's idea, however.

She is not the sort of woman Arthur ever imagined when he imagined lust. Tall, with big breasts, high hips, a heavy behind, she has steel-gray hair which she wears piled on her head, stuck randomly with bobby pins. Her face is rubbery and slightly squashed-looking. Her clothes are uniformly stretchy; they smell of dog. And still, Arthur feels for her an attraction stronger than any he has felt for any woman in his life, even Claire. He wonders if this is grief, insatiable grief, masquerading as lust to trick him, or spare him something. Sundays he lies all day in Eva's bed, reading the copies of *Dog World* and *Dog Fancy* which cover the floor. He can identify any breed now, from Chinese Crested to Owczarek Nizinny, from Jack Russell Terrier to Bichon Frisé. She has infected him with her expertise.

And now Mrs Theodorus gently nudges him, points to Mrs Jaroslavsky, who sits across the table. She knits. He sees stitches being counted and measured in the raising of eyebrows, the slight parting of lips. He once read that all human gestures, if filmed in slow motion, can be shown to be co-ordinated with sounds, and he is trying to see if Mrs Jaroslavsky's eyes and lips are indeed pursing and opening to the calm voice of Olivia, the social worker. Olivia's voice is like water, and so is her bluish hair, which falls down her back in an effortless ponytail.

Christa, tears in her eyes, tells the group, 'If he makes me wait three hours again tomorrow, I don't know – I'll just give up.' She shakes her head. 'I'm ready to give up,' she says. 'I stare at the stupid fishtank,' she says. 'I read Highlights for Children. Sometimes I just want to say to hell with it.'

Collectively, the members of the group have spent close to three of the past ten years in doctors' waiting rooms. Cheerily, Bud Israeloff reminds everyone of this statistic, and the group responds with a low murmur of laughter. Only the spouses are silent. They sit next to their sick beloved, clutching hands, looking worriedly across the table to see whose husbands and wives are worse-off than theirs.

'We all understand, Christa,' Kitty Mitsui says. 'You know what happened to me once? I had to wait two hours in the waiting room, and then I had to wait an hour and a half in the examining room for the doctor, and then I had to wait another hour for them to take my blood. So when I heard the BR finally coming I pulled the sheet up over my face and pretended I was dead. It gave him a shock, I'll tell you.'

'What's a BR?' a new wife asks sheepishly.

'That's just group talk, honey,' responds a more experienced spouse. 'It means bastard resident.'

Olivia does not like to encourage this particular subject. 'Let's talk about what to do, practically, to allay waiting anxiety,' she says. 'How can we help Christa get through tomorrow?'

'One of us could go with her,' Kitty Mitsui says. 'Christa, do you play Scrabble?'

'I don't know,' Christa says.

'I could do it,' Kitty says. 'I've got the day off. I'll sit with you. I'll bring my portable Scrabble set. We'll play Scrabble, and when we get bored with that, we'll make origami animals. I know it's not much, but it's better than the fishtank.'

'Waiting to hear if I'm going to live or not, if I can have a baby,' Christa says, 'and they keep me in the waiting room. Christ, my life is on the line here and they make me wait.'

Under the table, Eva's hand takes Arthur's. He folds the note she has given him into quarters, then furtively reads it.

'Have you been putting the oil in her dinner?' Eva has written. 'You need to for her coat.'

It is decided. Kitty will go with Christa and Chuck to Christa's doctor's office tomorrow. She'll bring her portable Scrabble set. And now, that matter concluded, Iris Pearlstein takes the floor, and says, 'If no one minds, I have something I'd like to address, and it's this food. It's hard enough for me to come here without it looking like I'm at a barmitzvah.'

[45]

For once Mrs Jaroslavsky stares up from her knitting. 'What?' she says.

'This food, this food,' she says, and waves at it. 'It makes me sick, having to stare at it all night.'

'I just wanted to make things a little more cheerful,' Mrs Jaroslavsky says, and her mouth trembles. She puts down her knitting.

'Oh, who're you kidding, Doris? You want to make it more pleasant, but I'm sorry, there's nothing nice about any of this.' She looks at her husband Joe, broken by recent radiation, dozing next to her, and puts her hand on her forehead. 'Christ,' she says, lighting a cigarette, 'we don't want to stare at fucking cake.'

Arthur wonders if Mrs Jaroslavsky is going to cry. But she holds her own. 'Now just one minute, Iris,' she says. 'Don't think any of this is easy for me. When Morry was in the hospital, I was up every night, I was half-crazy. What was I supposed to do? So I baked. That food was the fruit of suffering for my dying husband. You know how it was. I kept thinking that maybe if I just keep baking it'll keep the clock ticking, thinking, God, for one more cake, give him six months.' She frowns. 'Well, God defaulted. Now Morry's gone, and my freezers are stuffed. The truth is I bake for all of you the way I baked for him. There's nothing nice about it.'

She resumes her knitting. Iris Pearlstein takes out a kleenex to blow her nose. Once again Mrs Theodorus takes Arthur's hand under the table. Mrs Jaroslavsky looks vibrant.

'Ask if you can take home the poppy seed,' Arthur reads when he unfolds Eva's note.

Arthur got the puppy when Mrs Theodorus offered the group a discount on her new litter. 'A pet can really cheer you up,' she explained at spouse night. 'Thehuman–animal bond is so important in this stressful world.'

After that, Arthur approached Mrs Theodorus and said, 'I might be interested in a puppy. Since Claire passed on – '

'I know, I know,' she said, and smiled. 'Come tomorrow, in the afternoon.'

He drove through a rainstorm. Mrs Theodorus lived in a small, sleek cobalt-blue house in a neighbourhood where the streets flounced into cul-de-sacs and children played Capture-the-Flag with unusual viciousness. The puppies stared up at him from their kitchen enclosure, mewing and rubbing against one another, vying for his attention. 'This little girl is the one for you,' Mrs Theodorus said, and he was amazed that she could tell them apart. 'Look at this.' She pried the puppy's mouth open, revealing young fangs.

'Looks okay,' Arthur said.

'Can't you tell?' said Mrs Theodorus. 'Her bite's off. She'll never show. A pity, because her coat's really good, almost as good as Alicia's was, and she's got the best bone structure of any of them.'

'Claire had a Yorkie named Nadine,' Arthur said. 'She died a few months before Claire did. I think I'm relieved.'

'Oh, I can't talk about the death of dogs right now,' Mrs Theodorus said.

He took the puppy home with him that day. Claire had been gone a week, and still he was finding things he could not bear – today it was a half-finished New York Times acrostic puzzle. It was three weeks old. Already her handwriting was shaky. Did she have any idea then, he wondered, that the rash creeping over her skin, that unbearable itchy rash, was going to kill her? He certainly didn't. You don't die from a rash. A rash would

[47]

have been embarrassing to bring up in group, where
hematomas and bone loss were the norm. Claire's bane,
her great guilt, in the group, was that she was one of the
healthier ones, but she hoped that meant she could
help. 'What the group does – what we mostly do – is
figure out how to help each other,' Arthur remembered
Claire saying, as the two of them sat at the kitchen table,
drinking coffee. She had just come back from her
second night at group. The third night she didn't come
back until four in the morning, and he went half-mad
with panic. 'We went to the Greek Tycoon's,' she explained blithely. 'Mr Theodorus bought us all drinks.'

The fourth night was spouse night, and he went.

He sat down at the kitchen table with the double-
crostic and tried to finish it; one of the clues Claire
hadn't been able to get was a river which ran through the
Dolomites, and he became obsessed with figuring it out,
but as soon as he saw how thick and strong his own
handwriting looked in comparison with the jagged, frail
letters of Claire's decline, he lay his head down on the
newsprint and wept. The puppy watched him from the
corner. When he got up, he used Claire's last puzzle to
line her pen.

Just before spouse night ends Kitty Mitsui announces
that she and Mike Watkins and Ronni Holtzman will be
going to Poncho's afterwards for margheritas and nachos.
'It'll be a good time,' she says half-heartedly. But everyone
knows she is fighting a losing battle. Since Mr Theodorus
died the after-group outings have lost their momentum.

Then, in the group's golden age, its giddy second
childhood, in the reign of Mr Theodorus, there was
wild revelry, screaming laughter in the hospital parking
lot, until finally Mrs Leon, a Mormon, brought up her
moral objections at group.

The next week Mr Theodorus arrived with a rubber dog's snout tied over his nose. That was the end of Mrs Leon, Claire reported afterwards to Arthur, her eyes gleaming. He smiled. It seemed that Claire's greatest ambition was to be fully accepted into that subgroup of the group which played Charades until four in the morning, drank, and drove all night, one Thursday, to watch the sun rise over Echo Lake, where Kitty Mitsui had a cabin. Claire reported it all afterwards – the wind on her cheeks, the crispness of the air, the glory of the mountain sunrise. They built a fire and lay bundled together in sleeping bags, five of them, like campfire girls, she said.

Claire believed until the end that she was peripheral, barely accepted. She believed that Spiro and Kitty and the others were going out together without her, excluding her from the best, the most intimate gatherings. This was ironic, for as Arthur learned after her death, Claire was, if anything, the group's spiritual center; without her it fragmented. Mournful couples went home alone on spouse night, the healthy clinging testily to the sick. Then Mr Theodorus died, and the group entered a period of adolescent turmoil. Furious explosions occurred; well-buried animosities were laid bare. For the first time the group included enemies, who sat as far across the table from each other as possible, avoiding each other's glances.

Arthur can't help but wonder sometimes if any of it was sexual; if Claire might have slept with one of the men. It's hard for him to imagine. Usually, when he tries to envision those post-group revels, or when he dreams about them, he sees only five bodies huddled in sleeping bags by a lake as dawn breaks. Sometimes he wakes up with itchy hands, and bursts into tears because he wasn't there.

When spouse night ends, Mrs Theodorus says to Mrs

[49]

Jaroslavsky, 'Doris, if you don't need it – well, I could sure use that spice cake. I have this important show judge coming over tomorrow.'

'Don't do me any favors,' Mrs Jaroslavsky says. She is grim-faced, puffy. Then, cautiously: 'You really want it?'

'If you don't mind. This judge is very powerful, and God knows, I could never bake anything like that. All I have around are these horrible black forest things Spiro's brother sends over, with ten pounds of synthetic whipped cream.'

'Terrible, the things they call a cake,' Mrs Jaroslavsky says, as, smiling, she hands Mrs Theodorus an aluminum-wrapped package.

They walk out to the parking lot together. 'I know when I've outstayed my welcome,' Mrs Jaroslavsky explains to Mrs Theodorus and Arthur. 'I know it's been too long. I feel I can talk about that with you two, since we're all in the same position. The rest of them, they're fickle. When Morry died, they couldn't have been nicer, they kept saying, Doris, anything you want, anything you want. Now they'd like to slap my face. And that Olivia. She gets my goat. Every day it's, "Stay as long as you need, Doris, anything you need, Doris," but I know the score. She'd like to get rid of me too.' She blows out breath, resigned. 'So this is it, Mrs Jaroslavsky,' she says. 'No more spouse night. The rest of the way you have to go it alone.'

'I know how you feel, Doris,' Arthur says. 'The group's my last link to Claire. How can I leave them? Toward the end, sometimes I think, they knew her better than I did.'

'Oh, but they don't, don't you see?' Mrs Jaroslavsky says. 'That's just their illusion. They have each other for a year, maybe a little more. But what I have to remember, what I must remember, is I had Morry a

[50]

lifetime.' She smiles, breathes deeply. 'The wind feels wonderful, doesn't it?' she says, and turning from Arthur, opens her face to the sky, as if to absorb the starlight.

Across the parking lot Kitty Mitsui calls, 'Hey, you guys want to come for a nightcap? Come on! It'll be fun!' She smiles too widely at them, as if she imagines that by sheer force of will she can muster the energy to bring the dead back to life.

Arthur smiles back. 'No thanks,' he says. 'You go ahead.'

'Suit yourself,' Kitty Mitsui says, 'but you're missing a big blow-out.' She has four with her, including Christa and Chuck. Clearly she is destined to become the group's perpetual cheerleader, unflagging in her determination to bring back the glory of the past with a few loudly-called out cries. Poor Kitty Mitsui. The rest of them had lives, but she's thirty-two and unmarried. The group is her life, and it will be her doomed nostalgia.

Mrs Jaroslavsky winces as Kitty's car roars off. 'That smell,' she says. 'That particular smell of burnt rubber. I remember it from Morry's room when he was dying. It must have been something in one of the machines. Now I smell it — and I can hardly keep myself standing up.' She looks at the ground, clearly cried out for an entire lifetime, and Arthur is suddenly grateful to have Mrs Theodorus, grateful for the nights they may spend together in her dog-hair-covered bed. He will lie awake, listening for occasional yelps from the kennel.

'What you need,' Mrs Theodorus says, 'is a puppy,' and Mrs Jaroslavsky's mouth opens into a wide smile. 'My dear girl,' she says, 'I'm allergic.' Her face, against the dark sky, expands into a comic vision of the moon, eager-eyed and white-faced.

When Claire died, Arthur arranged for her ashes to be scattered at sea. It was what she had wanted. Everyone in the group had decided what they wanted, 'b vs. c,' or burial vs. cremation, being one of the most popular discussion topics at the post-group gatherings. He and the children took the plastic vial of ashes out on a boat which they had to share with another family – a staunch couple named MacGiver who had lost their son, and who resembled the protagonists of 'American Gothic'. Arthur felt faintly embarrassed as the two families engaged in nervous small talk. The wind was too strong to go out to sea that day, the young captain informed them; the scattering would have to take place in the bay. Arthur, as he figures it now, went crazy; 'she said the sea,' he kept repeating to the captain, who in turn kept explaining, calmly and compassionately, that the wind situation simply made it impossible for them to go to sea. 'It's okay, dad,' Arthur's daughters told him. 'The bay's almost the sea anyway.' But he was adamant. 'I told her the ocean,' he kept saying. 'I told her she'd be scattered over the ocean.' He clutched the vial to his chest, while the MacGivers discreetly they did their own dumping, shaking the little plastic bag over the water as if it were a sand-filled towel. 'Mister,' the captain said, 'we're going to have to turn back soon.' It was getting to be dusk. Finally, miserably, Arthur said, 'Oh, the hell with it,' and without even warning his children (Jane was in the bathroom at the time) dumped the vial over the side of the boat in a rage. The ashes swirled into the water like foam, the big chunks plopped and sank instantly. Nothing was left but a fine powder of ash, coating the inside of the bag, and in a moment of turmoil and indecision Arthur bent over and touched his tongue to the white crust, lapped it up. He was crying wildly. Dismayed, the MacGivers pretended to look the other way, pointing out to one another the Golden Gate Bridge, Angel Island, Alcatraz.

At Mrs Theodorus' house, the puppy writhes on the floor, urinates, rolls onto her back. Her mother ignores her. 'It's the hormonal change,' Mrs Theodorus explains blithely. 'After a few months, the mothers don't recognize their offspring any more.'

'I think that's sad,' Arthur says, even though he doesn't quite believe it, and Mrs Theodorus shrugs and pours out coffee. 'In a sense, it's better,' she says. 'They're spared the sensation of loss.'

She looks out at the grooming table, empty now, but still festooned with Alicia's ribbons and silver cups and photographs of Mrs Theodorus posed with her prize bitch. Across the room the puppies she has left lie with their mother in various states of repose. Only Arthur's puppy wags her tail, and stretches her legs behind herself, barely holding herself back from her uninterested mother.

'I think they slept together,' Mrs Theodorus says now.

For a moment Arthur thinks she is talking about the dogs. 'All of them,' Eva goes on, and her voice is low. 'That night they went to Echo Lake.'

'Eva,' he says, 'why are you saying this?'

'Oh, I think it's pretty obvious,' she says. 'You see, there were things I overheard – on the phone.'

Arthur is surprised at how panicked he feels, and tries to hide it. 'What did you hear?' he asks finally – not wanting to sound too curious, though he is.

'I heard Spiro talking to a woman. A woman he was clearly – intimate – with. I think it was Kitty. But then again, now that I think about it, it might just as well have been Claire.' She is quiet a moment. 'It wasn't just

[53]

the two of them, if you know what I mean. So I thought I would ask you if you knew anything – '

'I don't know anything,' Arthur says. He stares up at the ceiling. 'And I don't want to know anything, Eva. I don't want to know another bloody thing about that group.'

'Don't sound so holier-than-thou, Arthur. The two of us aren't exactly being saintly in our loyalty to the memory of our lost loved ones. So what if Claire was lovers with Spiro? Look at us.'

'Claire is in the water,' Arthur says. 'Spiro is buried.'

'He wouldn't have had it any other way,' Mrs Theodorus says.

They are quiet for a few moments. In the bright light of the kennel he can see the portrait of Mrs Theodorus smiling with Alicia that hangs over the table. Mouth open, red tongue hanging, the dead dog stares. Did she know, when the picture was taken that in a year she'd be dead? Did Claire guess, that morning she woke up and said, 'My hands are itching, Arthur. Were we near any poison oak last night?' All it took was three short weeks, and she was fighting to live. What did the group matter then? He was an egotist, a child, to think that his losing Claire to the group was anything even close to tragedy, to think his suffering came anywhere close to hers.

'Oh, Arthur,' Mrs Theodorus says. Her voice is shaky across the table. 'I shouldn't impose my weird ideas on you. Since Spiro died, I just don't know what I'm saying or thinking, or where I'm going. I could have read a lot into that conversation, I realize now. It was hard to make it all out. I just think that if I knew – maybe I wouldn't feel so lost.'

'Neither of us exactly feels found,' Arthur says. 'Remember how that first night at group after Claire died, I almost hit Ronni Holtzman when she said she was sorry? What was I supposed to say to that? It's okay? Claire's not really dead? It wasn't your fault?'

'Oh, Arthur,' Mrs Theodorus says. 'I know how you feel.' But Arthur doesn't answer. To know how *Claire* felt – that is the knowledge he longs for: lying in that bed, skin cracked and bleeding, tubes in his kidneys, his lungs, his arms. That is what he wants, craves, lusts to know – that harsh condition by which Claire was taken from him. Isn't it the great lie of the living, after all, that grieving is worse, is anything near death?

Distantly he feels hands, lips on him. It is Eva, wanting, he supposes, to make love, and he obeys, allowing her to walk him into her bedroom. But in his mind he is still on that boat, clinging to the vial of Claire's ashes. 'All right, already,' is what he thinks he shouted, when the captain said they would have to leave, and in fury he threw to the water those ashes he had cradled in his arms, those ashes he had loved and lived with. His daughters, he is sure, still murmur together about 'Dad's awful moment,' 'Dad's terrible behavior,' but in truth he is still angry at how grief carped around on that boat, pretending to dignity. 'You have profaned the memory of our mother,' his daughter Jane said to him in the car – it was she who had been in the bathroom – and yet he knows he would do it again; he would throw those ashes over in graceless fury, again and again.

'Kiss me,' Eva says nervously. He takes her in his arms. Through the window, the moon illuminates Mr Theodorus' supply of aftershave lotion, hair tonic, shoe polish – a row of dark bottles lined up carefully, like sentries, guarding the way in.

ORION

Jeanette Winterson

Here are the co-ordinates: five hours, thirty minutes right ascension, (the co-ordinate on the celestial sphere analogous to longitude on earth) and zero declination, (at the celestial equator). Any astronomer can tell where you are.

It's different isn't it from head back in the garden on a frosty night, sensing other worlds through a pair of binoculars? I like those nights. Kitchen light out and wearing wellingtons with shiny silver insoles. On the wrapper there's an astronaut showing off his shiny silver suit. A short trip to the moon has brought some comfort back to earth. We can wear what Neil Armstrong wore and never feel the cold. This must be good news for star-gazers whose feet are firmly on the ground. We have moved with the times. And so will Orion.

Every 200,000 years or so, the individual stars within each constellation shift position. That is, they are shifting all the time, but more subtly than any tracker dog of ours can follow. One day, if the earth has not voluntarily opted out of the solar system, we will wake up to a new heaven whose vaulted dome will again confound us. It will still be home but not a place to take for granted. I wouldn't be able to tell you the story of Orion and say, 'Look, there he is and there's his dog Sirius whose loyalty has left him bright.' The dot-to-dot log-book of who we were is not a fixed text. For Orion, who was the result of three of the gods in a good mood pissing on an ox-hide, the only tense he recognised was the future continuous. He was a mighty hunter. His arrow was

always in flight, his prey, endlessly just ahead of him.
The carcasses he left behind became part of his past
faster than they could decay. When he went to Crete he
didn't do any sunbathing. He rid the island of all its wild
beasts. He could really swing a cudgel.

Stories abound. Orion was so tall that he could walk
along the sea-bed without wetting his hair. So strong he
could part a mountain. He wasn't the kind of man who
settles down. And then he met Artemis, who wasn't the
kind of woman who settles down either. They were both
hunters and both gods. Their meeting is recorded in the
heavens but you can't see it every night, only on certain
nights of the year. The rest of the time Orion does his
best to dominate the skyline, as he always did.

Our story is the old clash between history and home.
Or to put it another way, the immeasurable impossible
space that seems to divide the hearth from the quest.

Listen to this.

On a wild night, driven more by weariness than
common sense, King Zeus decided to let his daughter
do it differently: she didn't want to get married and sit
out some war while her man, god or not, underwent the
ritual metamorphosis from palace prince to craggy
hero; she didn't want children. She wanted to hunt.
Hunting did her good.

By morning she had packed and set off for a new life
in the woods. Soon her fame spread and other women
joined her but Artemis didn't care for company. She
wanted to be alone. In her solitude she discovered
something very odd. She had envied men their long-
legged freedom to roam the world and return full of
glory to wives who only waited. She knew about the
history-makers and the home-makers, the great division
that made life possible. Without rejecting it, she had

simply hoped to take on the freedoms that belonged to the other side. What if she travelled the world and the seven seas like a hero? Would she find something different or the old things in different disguises? She found that the whole world could be contained within one place because that place was herself. Nothing had prepared her for this.

The alchemists have a saying, *Tertium non data*. The third is not given. That is, the transformation from one element into another, from waste matter into best gold is a process that cannot be documented. It is fully mysterious. No one really knows what effects the change. And so it is with the mind that moves from its prison to a vast plain without any movement at all. We can only guess at what happened.

One evening when Artemis had lost her quarry, she lit a fire where she was and tried to rest. But the night was shadowy and full of games. She saw herself by the fire: as a child, a woman, a hunter, a Queen. Grabbing the child, she lost sight of the woman and when she drew her bow the Queen fled. What would it matter if she crossed the world and hunted down every living creature as long as her separate selves eluded her? In the end when no one was left, she would have to confront herself. Leaving home meant leaving nothing behind. It came too, all of it, and waited in the dark. She realized that the only war worth fighting was the one that raged within; the rest were all diversions. In this small space, her hunting miles, she was going to bring herself home. Home was not a place for the faint-hearted; only the very brave could live with themselves.

In the morning she set out, and set out every morning day after day.

In her restlessness she found peace.

Then Orion came.

He wandered into Artemis's camp, scattering her dogs and bellowing like a bad actor, his right eye patched and his left arm in a splint. She was a mile or so away fetching water. When she returned she saw this huge rag of a man eating her goat. Raw. When he'd finished with a great belch and the fat still fresh around his mouth, he suggested they take a short stroll by the sea's edge. Artemis didn't want to but she was frightened. His reputation hung around him like bad breath. The ragged shore, rock-pitted and dark with weed, reminded him of his adventures and he unravelled them in detail while the tide came in up to her waist. There was nowhere he hadn't been, nothing he hadn't seen. He was faster than a hare and stronger than a pair of bulls. He was as good as a god.

'You smell,' said Artemis, but he didn't hear.

Eventually he allowed her to wade in from the rising water and light a fire for them both. No, he didn't want her to talk; he knew about her already. He'd been looking for her. She was a curiosity; he was famous. What a marriage.

But Artemis did talk. She talked about the land she loved and its daily changes. This was where she wanted to stay until she was ready to go. The journey itself was not enough. She spoke quickly, her words hanging on to each other; she'd never told anyone before. As she said it, she knew it was true, and it gave her strength to get up and say goodbye. She turned. Orion raped Artemis and fell asleep.

She thought about that time for years. It took a few moments only and she was really aware of only the hair of his stomach that was matted with sand, scratching her skin. When he'd finished she pushed him off already snoring. His snores shook the earth. Later, in the future, the time would remain vivid and unchanged. She wouldn't think of it differently; she wouldn't make it softer or harder. She would just keep it and turn it over in her hands. Her revenge had been swift, simple and devastatingly ignominious. She killed him with a scorpion.

In a night 200,000 years can pass, time moving only in our minds. The steady marking of the seasons, the land well-loved and always changing, continues outside, while inside, light years move us on to landscapes that revolve under different skies.

Artemis lying beside dead Orion sees her past changed by a single act. The future is still intact, still unredeemed but the past is irredeemable. She is not who she thought she was. Every action and decision has led her here. The moment has been waiting like the way the top step of the stairs waits for the sleep-walker. She had fallen and now she is awake. As she looks at the sky, the sky is peaceful and exciting. A black cloak pinned with silver brooches that never need polish. Somebody lives there for sure, wrapped up in the glittering folds. Somebody who recognised that the journey by itself is never enough and gave up spaceships long ago in favour of home.

On the beach the waves made pools of darkness around Artemis's feet. She kept the fire burning, warming herself and feeling Orion grow slowly cold. It takes some time for the body to stop playing house.

The fiery circle that surrounded her contained all the clues she needed to find that life is for a moment in one shape then released into another. Monuments and cities would fade away like the people who built them. No resting-place or palace could survive the light years that lay ahead. There was no history that would not be rewritten and the earliest days were already too far away to see. What would history make of tonight?

Tonight is clear and bright with a cold wind stirring the waves into peaks. The foam leaves slug trails in rough triangles on the sand. The salt smell bristles the hair inside her nostrils; her lips are dry. She's thinking about her dogs. They feel like home because she feels like home. The stars show her how to hang in space supported by nothing at all. Without medals or certificates or territories she owns, she can burn as they do, travelling through time until time stops and eternity changes things again. She has noticed that change doesn't hurt her.

It's almost light, which means the disappearing act will soon begin. She wants to lie awake watching until the night fades and the stars fade and the first grey-blue slates the sky. She wants to see the sun slash the water. But she can't stay awake for everything; some things have to pass her by. So what she doesn't see are the lizards coming out for food or Orion's eyes turned glassy overnight. A small bird perches on his shoulder trying to steal a piece of his famous hair.

Artemis waited till the sun was up before she trampled out the fire. She brought rocks and stones to cover Orion's body from the eagles. She made a high mound that broke the thudding wind as it scored the shore. It was a stormy day, black clouds and a thick orange shining on the horizon. By the time she had finished, she was soaked with rain. Her hands were bleeding, her hair kept catching in her mouth. She was hungry but not angry now.

The sand that had been blonde yesterday was now

brown with wet. As far as she could see there was the grey water white-edged and the birds of prey wheeling above it. Lonely cries and she was lonely, not for friends but for a time that hadn't been violated. The sea was hypnotic. Not the wind or the cold could move her from where she sat like one who waited. She was not waiting; she was remembering. She was trying to find what it was that had brought her here. The third is not given. All she knew was that she had arrived at the frontiers of common sense and crossed over. She was safe now. No safety without risk, and what you risk reveals what you value.

She stood up and in the getting-dark walked away, not looking behind her but conscious of her feet shaping themselves in the sand. Finally, at the headland, after a bitter climb to where the woods bordered the steep edge, she turned and stared out, seeing the shape of Orion's mound, just visible now, and her own footsteps walking away. Then it was fully night, and she could see nothing to remind her of the night before except the stars.

And what of Orion? Dead but not forgotten. For a while he was forced to pass the time in Hades, where he beat up flimsy beasts and cried a lot. Then the gods took pity on him and drew him up to themselves and placed him in the heavens for all to see. When he rises at dawn, summer is nearly here. When he rises in the evening, beware of winter and storms. If you see him at midnight, it's time to pick the grapes. He has his dogs with him, Canis Major and Canis Minor and Sirius, the brightest star in our galaxy. Under his feet, if you care to look, you can see a tiny group of stars; Lepus, the hare, his favourite food.

Orion isn't always at home. Dazzling as he is, like

some fighter pilot riding the sky, he glows very faint, if at all, in November. November being the month of Scorpio.

THE NIGHT
THE BLOOD

Damon Galgut

Kevin and Kyle at the side of the pool. Next to each other on reclining chairs, arms at their sides. They have glasses beside them and Kevin wears shades.

It's a hot day, late afternoon, and clouds are building in the West. But above them the sky is clear and very big: Africa. Kyle lifts a hand to shade his eyes. 'Gonna rain,' he says. He drops his hand.

'Ja.'

'Not much sun left. Gonna hit the clouds in a little while.'

'Can see.'

'Wanna swim? Last time.'

'Naah.'

Kyle stands and walks to the edge. He isn't wearing a costume (Kevin is) and his bum is white. He carries in his flesh the mark of the wicker chair, like the impression of a secret grief. He tests the water with his toe.

'Warm?'

'As blood,' he says, and grins.

Kevin smiles back. For a moment it is like this with them: a pair of boys in the dying light, showing their teeth in open smiles, at ease; in love. Then Kyle, he turns away.

He's a tall boy, Kyle, higher than Kevin by the top of his skull. His hair is brown. He has a pleasant face: large eyes, clear brows. His mouth is small, with gentle lips. There is that in his face, and in all the lean length of his body, that speaks of gentleness. He has never harmed

[69]

anyone. He has never had to fight; to carry out an injury in his own defence.

Kevin is a fighter. There is no thinness in him. His face is dark and narrow, the small bones pinched on some inner conflict that he cannot express. Words, it seems, are in flight in him; beneath the dark armour of his face. His mouth is tight: a tense arrangement of lips and teeth. Now, as he watches Kyle, his tongue emerges: pink as a wound, it touches on the stubble at the side of his mouth and is gone.

Summer in the high air: above the trees, the sky is rippling with heat. Kyle dives, launching himself from the side of the pool into momentary flight. A pink trajectory, he strikes the surface and disappears.

Under the water, tied up, it seems, in bubbles as white and round as stones, Kyle knows that he will sleep with Kevin tonight. The water, indeed, is warm and sleek as pulsing blood: his own, his own. He swims.

They met a year ago, at the university on the hill. Sitting next to each other at the same lecture, they had got to talking. They liked each other. They found one another amusing. Kyle was from up-country, a thousand kilometres away. The city was strange to him, as was living here, a long way from home. He loved his parents, his house; with pangs he recalled the garden in which he'd grown up. The mountains; the trees. Kevin came from the city; was bitter with life. He disliked his home, his sisters; the territory presided over by his mother, the despot, whose iron-grey hair invaded his dreams. He wanted to move, to dwell in other places; but his mother kept him where he was. He had to study, she told him, in order to make a living. Like his father before her, who resided now beneath a rectangle of turf in an exclusive acre on the hill, she was a woman of means. She placed store by status, and had trained him to do the same.

The boys became friends. United by their isolation, they took comfort in each other. Young and unhappy, they went everywhere together. They sat between lectures. They went to the beach. Once in a while they would walk up the mountain and smoke dope. At such times they felt able to share their most intimate secrets. Drugged and at ease, they giggled over calamities that had beset them in life. Jealousy; rage; fear. When he was younger, Kyle had been caught stealing cash. 'I cried,' he said.

'I watched my mother changing once.'

'I ran away from home when I was small.'

'I jerk off twice a day.'

They laughed.

Till on a day, as the sun went down behind the crest of the mountain above them, Kyle stared at Kevin and told him:

'Queer. Me.'

There was a pause.

'I mean, I like boys. Guys. I think.'

'For how long . . . have . . .'

'Always,' said Kyle. It was true: he always had. Growing older in his small home town, as his body changed shape, this other shape remained in him, like the outline of his shame. In him there was a dark and tangled need that filled his limbs like blood.

'I've never told anyone before.'

'Why did you tell me?'

'Because I . . . I wanted to tell you.'

'I'm glad,' said Kevin, ill-at-ease, 'I'm glad you felt you could.'

But he was not glad.

They did not mention this fact between them again.

[71]

As if nothing had been said, they resumed their lives and their friendship. In walking and talking, in the odd, accidental caress, the months were passed away.

Winter came. It rained. The fog drew down in blue and heavy folds. And Kevin found a girl-friend: tall and elegant as Kyle, with red hair tied behind her head like hands. Her name was Kim. Regal and calm, this Kim arrived between them like a force. She held Kevin's hand. She stroked his neck. They went everywhere together: to plays, to films, to the shops on a Saturday morning. She was a woman in control, was Kim, and she did not like Kyle.

'I hope you don't mind,' said Kev. 'I have to spend time with her, you see.'

'Yes,' said Kyle. 'Of course I see.'

'It is difficult for me to be in love.'

'Yes,' said Kyle. 'I know.'

He did not mind. He understood. It was, as he knew, a difficult thing, and Kim was a respite for his friend.

In truth it was easier for Kevin to touch him, now that the woman was here. Where before he was distant, now he came close. He was absolved. When they did see each other (usually late at night, when Kevin popped round to his tiny room), they would sometimes hug each other. And sometimes, just in talking, Kevin would take his hand. Between them was a gentle thing that neither of them could name.

Once, Kevin kissed him: a soft short pressure on his lips. 'Because you're good,' he said.

They smiled at each other.

In time, Kyle grew at ease. Kevin ennobled this need in him, so that what he had first felt to be unbearable darkness in himself, was light. He told his friends. At the end of the first term, on holiday at home, he called his parents into the study and made his confession to them. They did not seem upset, though his mother did cry. She took his hands in hers and kissed him on the cheek. 'As long as you're happy,' she said.

'Yes,' said his dad. 'That is all I can hope: that you're happy.'

He was. He found it in him to be happy with this: a love of all men, and one in particular.

Kevin was the only constant presence in his life. In the name of friendship, they would touch: the hugging of arms. The holding of hands.

(And that one, that solitary kiss.)

For Kyle could see in Kevin what most could not: the most private of pains that kept him tossing in his bed at night. Kevin concealed his need. His mother, with her iron-grey hair, would not understand this terrible vice in him. She would not wish him well. She was a woman incapable of happiness herself and would not approve it in him. Happiness was not a part of any life: much less his own, with its dreadful routine of learning and labour. He did work hard, to hide his hurt: from his mother, from himself. He studied. He slaved. He visited Kim. He gave her gifts.

He brought her home to meet his mother. They got on well, these two, in the way of powerful women: holding hands, they would stroll on the lawn. From behind the white curtain in the lounge, Kevin watched. They walked together. They laughed. In the blinding light of the garden it was hard, sometimes, to tell them apart. Lanky and tall, Kim was a mother as well. Her hair would also be grey.

But he loved her, he thought, as best he was able. He could not touch her without being hurt. But he forced himself to kiss her, to put his tongue inside her mouth. She would respond at times like these, throwing her awful limbs about him like a trap. They rolled on the floor. There, in the private prison of her home, she would take his clothes off him and go over the surface of his body with her hands. She sucked him with her lips. He would endure these times as a kind of price: the price he had to pay for her; her company; her name. They got on well.

It was only at the slightest of moments that he gave himself away. He would catch an occasional glimpse of himself in the mirror and give a start: he wore cravats. He wore bright shirts. It was in these, in the colour of his clothes, that his heart was most visible. He would stop then, in front of the glass, and stare at his face until there was nothing in it that could be called girlish. Or soft.

And he would change his clothes.

He went to the gym. He took up running. With muscles and sweat he tried to erase this other version of himself that he carried within. To an extent he succeeded: his body was stronger. With pride he saw that he was bigger than Kyle, that his shoulders were broader. He walked, he believed, with a heavier tread.

'There's something wrong,' his mother told him one evening, as they sat at the table for dinner. 'With Kyle.'

'Wrong?'

'He's not normal. I'm telling you. After a bit you learn to see.'

'Wrong?' he said again. He stared at her.

'Kim also thinks so. We've talked about it.'

'What?'

'He's one of *those*,' his mother said, and flapped her withered hand.

He spoke to Kim about it that night, or on the day after. 'What makes you think . . .?'

'Oh, Kevin,' she said, and tossed her head. 'A woman can see. He doesn't have a girl-friend, does he?'

[74]

'That doesn't mean a thing.'

'Oh, but it does. It does. He hangs round you all the time. Can't you see? It isn't right.'

'I don't mind,' he said, lying to her.

'Why don't you mind? People,' she said, and blew from her mouth a gust of dark smoke, 'people will *think*.'

'Let them think. Let them.'

He was thinking himself.

That same night, after visiting Kyle in his room on the way back home, he kissed him again. He left without looking back.

At the end of the winter, as a strong new spring came creeping from the ground, Kim left him for an Italian man with a scar and a Porsche. 'It's seasons,' she told him. 'They get in my blood. I have to change. You know?' He knew. Overcome with relief, he went to Kyle's room and sobbed out his heart. 'I loved her,' he cried. 'She was the only person I've ever loved.' And Kyle took pity on his friend. He patted his back. He lay beside him on the bed and whispered consolations in his ear.

Later, when Kevin was calm again, they sat on the floor and drank coffee. 'I have something to tell you,' Kyle said. 'I am in love with you.'

'I know you are,' said Kevin. 'But I'm not in love with you.'

'I think you are.'

'How can you say that? How can you . . .'

'That is what I see.'

'I'm not. Listen, Kyle, I'm not. I don't feel what you feel.'

They stared at each other in the flickering light.

'All right,' Kyle said.

They did not touch again.

[75]

After this, Kevin was given to bouts of temper for no apparent reason. Once, when Kyle had bumped him accidentally in passing, he lashed out with his fist. He hit Kyle on the jaw. 'Oh jeez,' he said. 'I'm sorry.'

Kyle was staring. 'What,' he said, 'is the matter?'

'Nothing. Nothing. It's just . . . you,' he ended softly. 'You're everywhere,' he said.

'I'm not. I hardly ever see you these days.'

'I have to spend time with my mother. She needs me now.'

'Why now?'

'If you have to know, it's the anniversary of my father's death next month. Okay?'

'Okay,' said Kyle and turned away.

He'd never laid eyes on Kevin's dad, but had seen him in photos: along the walls of their huge and desolate house, these grainy pics were hung. Granular, smudged, the visage of this unknown man looked down.

'His name was Kevin too,' explained the mother of his friend. 'He was married once before he married me.'

'Oh.' Kyle smiled at her.

She only looked at him.

She did not like him, this angular woman in whom the bones were showing. She glared at him when she saw him. He had often turned to find her studying him. Her eyes were loveless, large and cold. Her hands were heavy with rings.

He asked her once, when Kevin was upstairs, bathing. 'You don't like me to come here.'

'I don't mind,' she said.

'No, tell me. I've been taught to be direct, you see. You don't like me to be with your son.'

'I think,' she did finally concede, 'that you see too much of him.'

'Why? We're friends, after all.'

[76]

'I don't,' she told him, drawling with dignity, 'I don't want to discuss it further.'

And she retreated into the house behind, her long dress trailing like blood.

There were moments, too, when his own patience ran thin: he could not bear the pressure of his need. At these moments he would snarl:

'Christ, Kevin, what is the matter? It isn't wrong, you know, to feel like we do . . .'

'I've told you, Kyle. Can't you understand? I don't love you the way that you love me.'

'How, then? Tell me. How do you love me, Kev?'

'Like a . . . I dunno. A brother, Kyle. A friend.'

'Friends don't feel the way we feel. Friends don't lie in bed the way we do –'

'But why shouldn't they? There's nothing wrong with that. Is there? Is there?'

And Kyle, defeated, shook his head.

Summer came down: a yellow shock. Kevin had another girl-friend, but she didn't last. Kyle and Kevin went to movies; took walks together in the afternoons. They studied together as exams drew near. On one such day, in Kyle's cramped room all strewn about with books, Kevin bent in passing and kissed his friend on the back of the head. 'I'm sorry,' he said. Kyle's hand came up and touched his neck. The boys embraced: a long hug, close. Their hearts were pounding in their chests.

It was soon after this that Kevin's mother came to him. She shut the door of his room behind her and waited, thin arms folded across her chest. 'I have to talk to you,' she said.

'What about?'

'About your friend. What is it,' she demanded, 'that is going on?'

[77]

'How? Where? What do you mean?'

'You know, Kevin, what I mean. Not so? What is happening between you and that boy? Tell me. I want to know.'

'Nothing,' he whispered, 'cos his throat was dry.

'Tell me.'

'Nothing,' he said, and stared at her.

Till she went away.

At the height of the season, when the year was done, the two boys went north in a borrowed car to where Kyle lived. They stayed for two weeks. It was on the last day there, as the afternoon waned, that they found themselves at the side of the pool, immobile in the sun.

As Kyle dries himself with a towel, the sun goes down behind the clouds. A shadow falls across the boys and, as it does, a wind comes up. It is suddenly cold.

'Time to go,' says Kyle.

'Yep.'

They gather their things. Kyle puts on his costume again and picks up the empty glasses. 'What about the chairs?' says Kev. 'Leave them,' Kyle shrugs; and they go, hurrying from the high plateau of lawn as the dark comes down.

Kyle's parents are away, called to a farming convention in town. So the cottage is empty below them, standing white and lightless in the gloom. They hurry down the unseen path, while the trees are roaring about them; leaves go blowing across the track.

Inside, they lock the door. 'Jeez,' says Kevin, out of breath. 'We better shut the windows.' And they do, hurrying away on separate missions in silence. Kyle goes to the upstairs rooms, Kev takes downstairs. There are shutters on the windows. They must be closed and barred.

When they have finished, the house is utterly still,

though they can hear the wind outside. It is dark now, though evening has still to come. Kyle goes downstairs to where Kevin is waiting, standing in the lounge with his hands at his sides. They look at each other across the room. Neither will move.

'It's dark,' says Kev at last.

'I can't see you.'

'Nor you.'

There is a pause.

'It's kind of strange.'

And Kevin agrees.

Then Kyle walks slowly across the room to where Kevin is. He touches his face with the back of his hand. Then he kisses his friend on the mouth; and this time he doesn't stop. They fall to the ground. They get undressed. Kyle atop Kevin; Kevin on Kyle. In the darkening room, with the wind growing louder and the rain beginning to fall, they are touching each other in intimate ways and twisting on the floor.

When Kevin does come, it is with a burst of endless pain: a jet from within that tears from his heart these images of love: his friend, his friend, this boy, without whom he cannot do . . . he cries . . .

And it is only after, when Kyle has got up and put on the light, that Kevin, still lying where he was, can look down at himself and see with growing horror in his brain that what has come pouring from him is a huge and sticky pool of blood.

Kyle drives him to the doctor's rooms in town. 'He's a family friend. He won't mind at all.' But Kevin will not allow him to come up. He sits and waits in the empty car, while the rain hisses down in silver sheets of pain.

Dr Noble stares at Kevin. 'New in town?' he asks, smiling slightly.

'Visiting friends.'

'Oh. Who? Is it anyone I know?'

'No,' says Kevin. 'No.'

'What seems to be the trouble?'

Kevin takes a breath. 'It's embarrassing, doctor.'

'I hear all sorts of stories.'

And they laugh together.

'I had an orgasm,' Kevin tells him. 'And blood came out.'

Dr Noble is concerned. 'When did this happen?'

'Now—now, just before I phoned.'

'We'd better take a look.'

Kevin undresses in the other room. Naked for the second time tonight, he lies down on the couch to await the doctor. On his stomach and thighs are the faintest traces of red that he could not wash off.

Dr Noble comes in, sleeves rolled and arms bare. Onto his right hand he is pulling a glove: transparent, plastic. 'Now then,' he says. 'Relax.'

Kevin sits as he is directed: knees up, back straight. The doctor inserts a finger into him, probing the reaches that, only an hour ago, Kyle had touched. It hurts. And Kevin has to close his eyes to stop himself from crying.

'I'm so ashamed,' he says at last.

'I'm sorry,' Dr Noble says, and smiles at him in genial misunderstanding.

Then the examination is over.

'It's nothing,' Dr Noble says. 'Nothing serious at all. Look,' he says. 'It happens to people. A blood vessel here,' he taps his groin, 'it bursts, and blood comes out. No more than that.'

Kevin stares in disbelief. That may be what the doctor believes, but he knows (he *knows*) the truth of this event: the horror of a love for which his blood is due.

[80]

'Thank you,' he says.

'You may get dressed.'

He does. He passes close to the window of the room and catches a glimpse of Kyle, waiting and alone, in the steaming street below. He tries not to shudder.

As he leaves, he shakes the doctor's hand. His grip is firm and very cool: the grasp of a man. 'Thanks for coming in so late.'

'Were you with someone when this happened?' Dr Noble lifts a brow.

Kevin shakes his head. 'No,' he says. 'No.'

At the door he turns and adds: 'I was on my own.'

He goes down the stairs to where his lover is waiting.

It will not be the same after the night the blood came out of him. They will never touch each other again with any intent. They will drive back the next day to the city where Kev lives, and Kyle will drop him at his home. His mother, with her iron-grey hair, will be there, awaiting, and will clasp him to her iron breast as fiercely as she did when he was truly young. And they will go inside together, arm in arm.

Kyle will go back to his dingy flat, where Kev will never come again. He will sit there on his own and think.

In time, of course, our Kev will take another girl: a buxom lady, built of bricks. Her name is Lynette. With her hairless arms and long shaped nails, she will woo Kevin from his mother's grasp. She will give him romance. They will go everywhere together. They will, before long, share a flat in town. Between them, they will throw parties to which a great many people are invited. And in a few years (who knows?), our Kev may even marry her. He will not be entirely happy, but he will not care. There is a sanity to this, you see: when he gives to her his love, his blood is not involved.

[81]

Kyle will have other lovers. He will find a peace of mind. But, in the years to come, among the many faces he will meet, he will think from time to time of one particular boy; and how in this life it is possible to lose what one has never really had.

THE HOUSE
OF FUNERALS

Lawrence Scott

The morning sun blazed down hot on to the small, rusty-roofed houses with filigreed, white, lattice-work verandahs, yellowing. Fern baskets, hanging from eaves festooned with cobwebs, dripped.

The tumble-down town tumbled down to the wharf in the bay on the gulf and jangled with Indian music. On the High Street loudspeakers blared from the doorways of Ramnarine's Garment Palace and shattered the glass cases in Patel's Jewel Box.

The sea in the bay on the gulf glinted.

Above the traffic and the commerce of the town, on top of the hill with the fir trees, the jangle achieved a monotony. The heat, like a mirage, floated above the pitch road cut into the ochre earth winding up the hill.

On the gulf the mirage hung above the glinting, clamped downfast, leaden lid of the sea; the grey lid of an ancestral vault.

The jangling tumbled-down town, the sweating morning, the jalousies-shuttered room behind Teresa's Hairdressing Salon to which Gaston, the grandson of Cecile Monagas went 'to play in the dirty water with that coolie girl' as his mother would say, the grave-diggers in Paradise Cemetery, the women in the flower shop entwining sweet-lime bushes into wreaths with tuberoses and catalair orchids, the women of the Legion of Mary and Father Sebastian the parish priest, all waited expectantly for the news that Cecile Monagas de los Macajuelos had eventually died.

Now on top of the hill in the garden with the fir trees
there was the house: a vantage point from which to see
the plains seeping from the swamps towards the conti-
nental cordillera of mountains in the north; the cocoa
hills, ridged and green like the back of an iguana, rising
and falling across the centre of the island; the dusty
fringes of sugarcane disappearing into the southern
forests, black with oil – the blue-stone house in the
garden with the fir trees overlooking the gulf; each
blue-stone quarried from the cliffs near the sea on the
north coast of the island and brought to the top of the
hill by African men, women and children: overseered,
cajoled and sometimes paid weekly by Carlos Monagas
de los Macajuelos; watched by Madoo the nightwatch-
man, the son of an indentured labourer, so that the
people in the shacks below the hill would not steal the
bricks and iron rods for the foundations in order to
build their own fragile huts in the shadow of the blue-
stone house; in the shadow and the shade of its court-
yards, terraces, staircases leading to sunken gardens of
roses and anthurium lilies growing beneath mango trees
– the house with the grotto of the Blessed Virgin Mary at
the end of the path near the calabash tree whose interior
was cool with ferns potted in damp black earth and
palms growing beneath arches and under alcoves in
whose recesses there were busts of Venus and other
goddesses: floors of polished parquet, mahogany
chairs, tables, marble-topped chests of drawers from
the sale of Napoleon the Third's palace, crystals and
china in cabinets, portraits on the walls. In the bedroom
of the house above the orchid house at whose windowsill
she used to stand and watch the gulf and pray to the

Virgin, Cecile Monagas de los Macajuelos died at dawn. She had been dying for years.

'Poor dear. Mariana my child this is the end of an era.' Marie-Claire, the sister of Cecile, stroked the hair of her niece. They touched their eyes with embroidered, linen handkerchiefs, blotting the first tears.

The purple, pink, white and gold blooms which perched like carnival butterflies upon the rubbery leaves growing out of the dry logs encrusted with dry moss, hung from wires in the orchid house, rotting.

Carlos Monagas, Cecile's husband, had grown them and then died from inhaling nicotine and the fungal dust.

Carlos had died at Pentecost and the church had to be stripped of its festive red and draped in black for the requiem. The vases of red exhoras were banked in the sacristy.

He was buried in the ancestral grave beneath the marble angel with the broken arm. Someone had wanted to steal the bouquet of lilies from the clenched fist of the messenger of heaven.

Cecile then began to die. Carlos her rock of Gibraltar had sunk into the gulf or that is what her sister and family thought. 'This will be the end of Cecile.' What they saw sitting near to the casket like one of Carlos' orchids, white and wearing a purple dress, was a stunned Cecile. Like a butterfly which, buffeted and knocked suddenly to the ground as suddenly takes to the air for a day, to freedom: Cecile's freedom was like that of the butterfly.

She bought a car and could be seen at all parts of the island recording the changing landscapes of both the dry and wet seasons; holding on for dear life to her easel as she faced the windswept ocean raging in from off the Atlantic, so that she could depict the last detail in the

yellowing frond of a coconut tree, bent to the brink of
the water with its crown twisted back towards the land
by the force of the wind. She became daring and swore
at the sky which resisted being captured in a drop of
coloured water on her white pad. 'They change so
quickly,' she used to say, stamping her feet. She could
be found in remote country villages painting the shacks
of the poor and village women with baskets on their
heads.

Her enthusiasm for life was so intense after the death
of Carlos that she would come home quite amazed at the
happiness of the world. 'Why is everyone smiling and
waving at me today on the way back from Mass? The
town was so happy as I was going down High Street.'

'But Mummy, you're mad. High Street is a one way
street, an up street.'

'Don't tell me that dear. It could only be Saint Christopher and the hosts of guardian angels who saved me.'

She broke traffic lights in her eagerness.

But this burst and last claim on life was as short-lived
as the life of a butterfly because the pain and endurance
of the years had already destroyed her nervous system.
Her last paintings became abstract as she could no
longer control her fingers. They were splodges,
blotches; the bursting of atoms, molecules, elemental.
The water and the paints on the windowsill dried up.
The last entries in her diary were dots, waiting, trying
to steady her fingers.

The tinkle of the viaticum alerted Marie-Claire and
Mariana as Father Sebastian entered the house of funerals followed by the acolyte with the bell and the bucket
of holy water. Alicia the old nurse followed behind.

The women worked fast fearing putrefaction. They
washed the thin, dead limbs of Cecile's body with soap
and water. She was dressed in a blue night-gown be-

cause blue is the colour of Our Lady. Marie-Claire shook her head remembering, 'Mariana, I can see her now.'

'Aunty don't start remembering. I don't want to know.'

Marie-Claire sprinkled eau de Cologne onto a linen handkerchief and dabbed the forehead of Cecile's body. Afterwards she put the handkerchief to her nose and shook her head. 'I can see her now. I can see her as a bride.'

'Mr Samaroo is coming for the body, Aunty, and Father Sebastian is here.'

'Yes dear. She died before she could receive communion, but now she is in His arms,' she whispered while stroking the limp hair on Cecile's head.

The women knelt and received the viaticum intended for Cecile. Father Sebastian broke the host into four parts with a crumb for the acolyte. 'This will help you on your way,' he chuckled. He anointed the body of Cecile Monagas de los Macajuelos with the extreme unction: her forehead, lips, ears, nose, eyes, and he stroked the finger-tips and the extremity of the toes.

'Mr Samaroo take care,' Mariana helped to lift her mother's corpse, 'don't let me down'.

'Madam?' Samaroo's had been preparing bodies for burial in San Andres since before the beginning of the century.

'I'm coming for Mummy at two thirty. The funeral in the church is at four o'clock.'

'Plenty time Madam.'

'The funeral in the church is at four o'clock and I don't want anything to interfere with that. You know how many funerals they have in this town.'

'Take care going down the steps,' said Mr Samaroo the professional.

[89]

'At twelve o'clock the women of the Legion of Mary will come and say the rosary and keep vigil. Then there is clothes. Aunty what I going to dress Mummy in now?' Mariana's voice cracked.

'We will think of something dear,' Marie-Claire followed behind the little procession down the stairs: Mr Samaroo and his attendant carrying the body helped by Mariana, Father Sebastian, the acolyte and Alicia. From the bay window of the staircase Marie-Claire could see the gulf.

The sea was like a slate in the vanishing dawn. 'So, Mr Samaroo, have your business finish on time.'

'Yes Madam. You want the body to leave the home at three thirty?'

'She has to leave from here. This is where she lived. This is where her children born and died. She buried them from here, though she believed that they had flown like angels across the gulf.' Mariana's voice trailed off.

'Yes Madam. I see what you mean.'

'Do you? That is more than I can see. But you understand. She is not going to fly out over the gulf; assumed into heaven body and soul this afternoon. So please do your business properly this morning. You see this heat. Take care the body smell.'

'Madam you know how we does do business. Since my great grandfather doing this thing. Okay boy, rest down here, open the hearse door.'

'Take care, she so frail,' Alicia keened.

All the time Marie-Claire muttered, 'May the angels of heaven take her in their arms to Paradise.'

'And the advertisement, Madam, since 1888 we working for people in distress and now we have these new methods from America.'

'All the same Mr Samaroo heat is heat.' When she was

a little girl her grandmother said that she looked as
delicate and pretty as a porcelain figurine on the dressing-table of Marie Antoinette. She had grown old giving
birth to sons.

The procession dispersed; Mr Samaroo with the
corpse and Father Sebastian's blessing.

'Father Sebastian, the bells, you won't forget to toll
the bells?' Mariana cried out to the priest.

'Quite right Mariana. Good of you to remember the
bells.' Marie-Claire turned to go into the house.

Alicia who was reputed to be a hundred years old
returned to the servants' quarters with her ancestry.
Her father had been an English overseer and her mother
an African slave. She came from Barbados to be nurse to
generations of Monagas children. In the courtyard outside her room she looked up to the sky, 'Miss Mariana,
Miss Mariana, corbeaux circling in the sky.'

At that moment a fast car with screeching tyres drove
up into the yard; skidding on the pods from the flam-
boyant tree. 'Oh god all yuh, get out me way nuh.' It
was Gaston, Mariana's son.

'Where have you been all night? In that dirty water
again?' Mariana turned to go into the house.

This was Gaston, grandson of Gaston Monagas de los
Macajuelos, great grandson of Gaston Monagas de los
Macajuelos from the matrilineal blood; the descendant
of caballeros and conquistadors with fat features and
dark shadows over his eyes. His shirt was open and gold
chains with medals of Our Lady of the Immaculate
Conception and Saint Christopher nestled in the hairs
of his chest. He was sweating. 'God all yuh, leave a man
alone nuh. Give a man a chance nuh.'

'Your grandmother died in the night and that is
where you spend the night, shaming me and your father
and the name of your family,' Mariana screamed.

'My father, shame?'

'Madam, son.' Alicia raised her eyes to the sky search-ing the circling corbeaux.

The bedroom above the orchid house overlooking the gulf was left to air. The bedspreads were pulled off and the mosquito net drawn back. Cecile had died on her marriage bed. It was made of saman wood, cut from a tree in the pasture of her father and grandfather's estate. The carpenter had built, under the instructions and design of her husband, a canopy giving her the shade which is given beneath those trees. It rose to a crown carved with wild English flowers from which hung the capacious folds of the fine mosquito net, like the train of her daughter-brides, or her own bridal lace, or that of her mother and grandmother before her.

It was a bed of births and deaths into which had soaked the amniotic water of the afterbirth, the blood of the womb and the vaginal tissue. It was the bed into which she had miscarried nine times: baptizing with water from the basin near her bed; with her own hands and prayers; in hope and faith the soul had already filtered like sunlight through muslin or a blue after-noon. She dipped her fingers into the salt of the am-niotic water and searched for tongues, ears, noses, fingers, and toes to anoint.

'Do you renounce Satan and all his works?' She asked and immediately whispered back to herself, 'I do.' She whispered again, 'And all his pomp?' Again, 'I do.' She spoke for the formless and speechless lips, wet between her legs, or which she pulled up to her breasts to suckle in hope; umbilically tied so that she was even more entitled to speak for them.

The little white satin-covered coffins which were lined with quilted taffeta were brought to this bedroom nine times for those rescued from limbo by the ministrations of Cecile Monagas de los Macajuelos.

Bells in the parish church of San Andres rang with joy nine times for the little angels assumed into heaven.

Marie-Claire pulled off the linen sheets; damp with the sweat of death. She looked at the bed and shook her head. They had all known and kept silent.

She remembered the convent girl in the dormitory hidden beneath the linen shroud to change her clothes; hiding from her own body, a child of nuns with crisp habits and linen veils.

They had all been so excited. 'We are going to give out Cecile's engagement,' her mother had announced on the verandah. She could see her now in the armchair near the ledge with the angel-hair ferns. She filled the chair with her broad hips sitting with her snow-white hair, the mending basket at her feet and the low mahogany table set with cups and saucers for tea. 'Carlos Monagas has been to see your father.' The old French family to be united with the old Spanish family; there was great excitement.

The grave of his ancestors was in the ancient city of San Jose de Orunya, where the river has run dry and the spirits float in the candlelit air on All Souls night.

Mrs de Lapeyrouse had dug deep into her chest for the old, soft lace of her own wedding dress. There was no time to wait for a dress from Paris. Carlos was leaving for South America. The wedding day would be within the month. Cecile wore gold on her wedding day. The lace had turned yellow; penetrated by moths.

Marie-Claire dusted the room. She paused at the window-ledge and stared out over the gulf. The images of her sister's girlhood rose to meet her from the leaden vault.

She had been so frail, so pale; like the white of

blanched almonds in her yellowing dress. Carlos had thought of her as an orchid; like the orchid that he had found near the bleached drift wood at Galeota.

Then the morning at the wharf when they all waited to say farewell and to board the old rusting steamer, La Concepcion. Marie-Claire remembered turning to her mother, 'Mother, what will she do? What does she know?'

'Carlos Monagas is a gentleman,' her mother smiled remembering her own wedding night at sixteen.

When Cecile returned from South America it was left to Father Sebastian to guide her soul and to bury the dead angels.

3

The afternoon stretched out into the eternity which Father Sebastian had prayed for. The traffic jam began to build up in the High Street. Gaston, Mariana's son, parked his fast car in the open gutter. He went into the back room at Teresa's Hairdressing Salon. As his mother would say, and Alicia deplore, 'to play in the dirty water', but his father, thumping him on the shoulder, would advise him, 'take care with them young Indian beti boy.' The loudspeakers proclaimed their bargains. The Indian music sang high in the telephone and electric wires strung out low over the emblazoned galvanised roofs. Zinc creaked and syncopated rhythms throbbed from taxis and transistors.

The verandahs dripped.

The sea crinkled like galvanised roofs into the blue afternoon which stretched like membrane over the skeleton of a mountain in Venezuela.

The time of Cecile Monagas lived on. It lived on in the linen sheets; washed in suds and sunned in the courtyard; shook and ironed by Alicia; folded and brought up on a wooden tray for her madam to count and arrange in the linen press on the landing at the top of the steps in the blue-stone house. Cecile Monagas' time lived on: her fingers lived on in the embroidery on the pillow cases; in the table-cloths bargained for on the front steps of the blue-stone house with the Syrian merchant who brought his suitcases from Lebanon; in the filigreed lace which ran through the brown fingers of Mr Khan from Madras; in the doily mats from Madeira brought by the Portuguese wholesaler who had climbed Mount Mora in the hot sun.

Cecile Monagas had lived her time. It was accounted for in the shopping lists recorded at the back of her diaries, each item costed: in the weekly checks of the linen to see that the servants had not been stealing; in the lists of the babies' layettes; nine layettes kept in tissue-paper and preserved in moth-balls, but sweetened with cus cus grass from Dominica. There were christening gowns which had never been worn, lace bonnets and skull caps. Her presence lingered on in the souvenirs of her honeymoon and other paraphernalia of a young bride.

Her time was in the arrangements of flowers which young brides remembered in the sanctuary on their wedding day and which startled first communicants by the perfume of the frangipani bouquets. These were the same first communicants who were instructed in their faith and remembered her like a second mother. She gave them, at seven years old, a profound initiation into the mysteries of the immortality of the soul; why Adam and Eve were banished from the garden of Eden by an angel with a flaming sword and why Eve would bring forth children in sorrow and pain; of mortal sin and how

far venial sin stretched; of efficacious grace; the in-
fallibility of the Pope; the transubstantiation of bread
into flesh and wine into blood; the ascension of the
Lord; His transfiguration and the assumption of His
mother, the Virgin, into heaven, complete with body
and soul. These truths, like the eternity of the afternoon; these words, possessed the time of Cecile Monagas; so intimately were they part of her that they kept
recurring on the lips of the old women of the Legion of
Mary that morning in the sacristy while they polished
the brass candle sticks which would stand on either side
of the black, draped catafalque on which the coffin of
Cecile Monagas would rest at the centre of the church.

Ever since early morning, when he had anointed the
body of Cecile Monagas, Father Sebastian had been
remembering her confessions. He alone possessed a
part of her which had now floated above the gulf into the
clear dawn of the distant mountains of Venezuela: her
invisible soul.

He remembered her, early, before the six o'clock
mass, in the line for the confessional.

'Bless me Father for I have sinned, Father it is one
day since my last confession.'

At first, he used to be surprised when he slid back the
varnished, latticed shutters, to hear the small voice of
Cecile Monagas yet again, when she had only been there
the morning before. But then he became accustomed to
her almost daily visits to him, as the representative of
her God, the judge and forgiver of her sins.

'My child there is no need for you to come each day.'
The priest felt that he had no other alternative but to try
and restrain her need to come to him each morning;
particularly when Cecile could not formulate precisely
the name of her sin and its dimensions, but only that she

carried about within her a sense of the enormity of sin
and that she was sinful by nature.

'My child, for your penance I want you to say your
daily rosary with special devotion for those souls who
are trapped in purgatory and for the sins of the world,
which weigh down upon the shoulders of our crucified
Lord and which pierce the heart of his Virgin Mother.'
He knew that these intentions would give her enormous
joy and purpose.

It took Cecile years to come to a formulation of her
sin. At first she thought that there were so many. Like
the story of the gospel: 'My name is Legion for I am
many.' She imagined her sin like little devils pricking
into her with their tridents, like the *jab molasse* at
carnival or the devils in the murals on the walls of the
convent. They were scruples which interrupted her
daily activities: that she hadn't kissed her husband's
cheek with sufficient fervour before he went to work;
she had not completed her mending; or that a crumb
had passed her lips inadvertently before going to the six
o'clock mass and she had received communion having
broken her fast; she had lost her temper with Alicia; she
felt too exhausted to play with the children; she had not
weeded the rose bed with Madoo and the bajac ants had
invaded on floating leaves upon the water in the anti-
formica clay pots and stripped leaves and petals from
Our Lady's roses. They arrayed themselves and invaded with such persistence. She had made a noise and
disturbed Carlos in the stillness of the orchid house as
she crushed the pebbles so they crunched and he was
rustled from his velvet scents, nicotine and the fungal
dust.

Her visits to Father Sebastian became more frequent.
She needed to see him before and after mass. She visited
him in his office in the presbytery, because during mass,

at the crucial moment of the consecration she was filled with a sense of sin; she remembered seeing her body in the mirror of the bathroom and so she was unworthy to receive the host.

Father Sebastian had to become more than just her parish priest and confessor. He became her spiritual director.

She gave him her soul: the most secret and immortal part of herself; into his hands, soft with blue veins; smelling of hosts, holy oils and incense. His breath always had a stale, sweet smell of the communion wine, the blood of Christ. She gave to him that part of herself she taught the children to take most care of in order to direct heavenwards away from the pit of hell and its scrupulous devils.

At lunchtime the women of the Legion of Mary went to Samaroo's to keep the afternoon vigil and to say the rosary. They arrived as the attendants wheeled out from the embalming room the prepared body of Cecile in its mahogany casket with simple brass handles and cross upon the lid. She was arranged in quilted satin like an artificial orchid in a plastic box you give loved ones on birthdays and anniversaries. Mariana and Marie-Claire had sent her purple lace dress. Mr Samaroo, with the power of all his art, skills and new methods from America, had arranged what little hair was left into a nimbus of silver curls.

In the presbytery Father Sebastian sat alone at the lunch-table gathering the crumbs of bread into little mountains. The fan on top of the corner cupboard whirred and swivelled, giving him an intermittent breeze. The water jug sweated dripping into the table-cloth. He squashed a soft grain of rice between his fingers. That morning he thought of crushed wheat and stamped grapes at the consecration.

In the orchid house below the bedroom of the blue-stone house the orchids on their logs were still rotting. The birds which were accustomed to sing and flick silver from the bird bath in their flight, had vanished into the sizzling stillness. The pipe in the orchid house dripped, filling the barrel so that it eventually over-flowed, and the water seeped through the pebbles to the underlying moss, all the time saturating the stone walls, growing with ferns, oozing into the beds with anthurium lilies, like a wet grave.

While the housekeeper did the washing-up Father Sebastian hung up his cassock behind the door of his bedroom and lay down in his vest and underpants beneath the whir of the ceiling fan. The Indian music from the bargain parade continued to advertise the seventy-five-per-cent discount in honour of the day, the coming weekend, the next weekend, the recession and the inflation. The picture of the Sacred Heart knocked against the wall in the hot air.

Gaston's car was still parked in the gutter with the dirty water running down the drain. He was still in the back room of Teresa's Hairdressing Salon.

The back room of Teresa's Hairdressing Salon kept its shutters closed so that the room sweated and the bedsprings creaked endlessly into the afternoon under the weight of Gaston's oppression. The weight of centuries humped into that ridiculous bottom. He had forgotten that it was the day that his grandmother had died but he kept remembering his father's advice 'take care with them beti boy' and understood that his father's advice had come from experience.

Father Sebastian had a distinct sense of loss.

The soul of Cecile Monagas had slipped through his consecrated fingers; young and nervous like a bride on her first night.

He imagined a young bird, fluttering, trapped in a house: the fear of the bird and the fear it engendered in the witness and perpetrator of its entrapment and in him, the person trying to free it, struggling with its rescuer. He was pained by the reverberations of its struggle and its attempt to find an open window.

In the last days it lay still as the body gave up living and the skin seemed to fade over the bones, transparent, so that the soul could slip through. When he anointed her body he did it in the belief that it had been a tabernacle.

The celibate had wooed her soul for Christ. Each morning she brought him her fear.

She had formulated her sin. She could not remember whether she had consummated her marriage.

'Father I can't remember. I am denying my husband his right.'

'My child look at your daughter.'

'But Father I pray to Our Lady of the Immaculate Conception.'

He attempted to remind her of the evidence of her life: her daughter who had lived; the baptisms she had administered; the memory of the nine little angels assumed into heaven. He reminded her of the taffeta-quilted, white satin coffins under the earth in Paradise Cemetery.

But each morning the amnesia returned as she woke with her heart fluttering like the wings of the trapped bird: waking with Carlos near to her before he left to descend to the orchid house for the morning inspection, but not being able to remember. There was a lid over her dreams, memories, as vast as the lid over the gulf; a grey shadow, the Holy Spirit brooding over the waters at the beginning of creation, overshadowing her.

Father Sebastian absolved her so that she could make

a new start, each day a new start to try and remember. Then Carlos had died.

Father Sebastian dozed off in his underpants and vest under the whirring fan as he reminded himself that he must tell the sexton to toll the bells.

The mourners began to arrive at the house standing about the yard in little groups; the relatives and the white friends. In the church the women of the Legion of Mary had begun the fifteen mysteries of the rosary.

The grave-diggers endured their vigil with tots of rum, leaning on their forks and spades sunk into the wet earth after they had tidied away the rotting planks of Carlos' coffin and overcome their astonishment at the remnants of the nine white satin coffins.

Alicia could not stay inside her room, battened down in the servants' quarters off the courtyard, outside the kitchen. There was no air. The trees did not stir and there was not a sound of a bird. There was only the monotony of the town and a little nearer the drip of the pipe in the orchid house. She dragged her stool under the arch which opened on to the path to the orchid house and the sunken garden. She liked to sit there because she could see the sea from there.

'So Madam gone,' she said to herself with her one hundred years. She stared at the sea and the swoop of the circling corbeaux over the gulf.

The wreaths began to arrive at the house and at the church piled up in the doorways, at the back of cars and on top of the hearse standing in the yard at the front of the blue-stone house; beginning to suffocate the atmosphere with the perfume of their dying blooms.

The women in the flower shops brushed up the wilting sweet-lime leaves and the dust of the asparagus fern.

Father Sebastian had woken and showered and put on a clean white cassock. He sat in his rattan rocker on the verandah of the presbytery behind the ledge with the pots of eucharist lilies reciting the Magnificat: 'My soul doth magnify the Lord'.

The Indian music, the transistors and the stereo taxis kept up their incessant screech and throb.

These last preparations for the obsequies of Cecile Monagas de los Macajuelos did not penetrate the sunless, shuttered and sweating room at the back of Teresa's Hairdressing Salon. Gaston had forgotten about his car parked in the gutter and that he was to be a pall bearer. It was creating a traffic jam in the High Street and no one had any idea whose it was, so careful had he been about his incognito. Two policemen kept walking around it, writing down the registration number and the number of the licence and tax disc into little black books and then walking away again. Taxi drivers shouted and gesticulated at it and pedestrians waiting for a taxi leant up on it allowing coca cola and curry juice from *barras* to drip on to it. None of this entered the emptied brain of Gaston. His activity had created a state of amnesia.

Marie-Claire had arrived back at the house in the same sweating afternoon to receive her sister's body from Samaroo's. She had powdered her nose and tidied her grey hair into a bun at the nape of her neck and wore a lilac dress. She had on a white hat with a tulle veil to blur her tears. She stood on the terrace with a cloud of blue plumbago and white Queen Anne's lace in front of her. She stared out over the gulf towards the mountains; the foothills of the Andes rising to the heights of Venezuela over the archipelago of linking islands, beyond the island of Patos.

'Aunty what you staring at?' Mariana called from the window upstairs. 'Mr Samaroo should be here any minute.'

'Just thinking dear.' She kept on staring, remembering. She remembered her mother and grandmother
whose ancestor rode on his horse beside Bolivar.

The leaden lid of the vault would once again open to
receive one of her own. She stared at the gulf.

The gulf stared back at her. This was the gulf into
which the ships with the slaves of Lopinot and Roume
St Laurent had sailed. This was the gulf into which had
sunk the burning galleons of Apodoca; the English,
French and Spanish ships of plunder. This was the gulf
into which had flowed the blood of suicidal Amerin-
dians claiming themselves in death rather than capture.
Into this gulf had flowed the disinfectant from off the
bodies of indentured Indians whose children and
women ate clay in the quarantine camps on the island of
Nelson. It was from the waters of this gulf that the
baptisms were administered to innocent people. And it
was along the shores of this gulf that a young black girl
of fourteen had strolled, smoking a cigar, and had later
been taken to an upper room in the port and tortured
with the chains of the Inquisition.

The gulf stared back, inscrutable and metallic.
Marie-Claire arranged a strand of stray grey hair behind
her ear and into the folds of her bun. She thought about
her own death.

Mr Samaroo delivered the coffin, lifting it carefully,
with the help of attendants, into the drawing-room
where the murmur of the rosary continued like the tide.
Five mysteries of the rosary were recited while the
relatives and white friends crushed through the front
doors into the hallway, overflowing on to the terraces,
until the house was once again a house for a funeral.
Women fanned themselves and the men mopped their
brows, sweating in their stuffed suits. Eau de Cologne
and Chanel No. 5 dripped in the perspiration.

[103]

'Where is that son of mine?' Mariana came and knelt near to Marie-Claire who was praying into the open coffin.

'Leave it in God's hands, my dear.' Marie-Claire continued with the rosary fingering the crystal beads.

'I wish I could say that he was in God's hands now, instead of you know whose arms.' Mariana stifled her anger out of respect for her mother and because she did not want to cause an embarrassment.

The five mysteries faded into the ejaculations for the dead. The pall bearers came to lift the coffin. Mr Samaroo, with generations of etiquette and respect, substituted for Gaston.

The doors of the hearse were shut and the last stages of Cecile Monagas de los Macajuelos' funeral procession began to wind its way slowly down from the top of Mount Mora; from the top of the hill with the fir trees in the garden of the blue-stone house overlooking the gulf. It descended, one car behind the other, behind the hearse: brakes creaking, bumpers almost scratching the chrome of the other; each car packed with family, weighted down and suffocating under wreaths stacked behind the back seats and on the bonnets. The procession descended into the jangling, tumble-down town: sweating, throbbing and locked in an inextricable traffic jam, because unknown to them all, family and friends, Gaston's car was holding up the traffic in the High Street, parked in front of Teresa's Hairdressing Salon.

Waiting in the church, the people of the town congregated: the black people who had known Miss Monagas; the women of the Legion of Mary both the Junior and Senior Praesidiums; representatives from the Catholic Youth Organisation; the first communion classes and the confirmation classes; the Catholic wing of the Girl

Guides and Boy Scouts; nurses from the Red Cross who had laboured over the body of Carlos Monagas; members of the Horticultural Society who had gone to the blue-stone house for orchid exhibitions; the Society of the Sacred Heart; children of Our Lady of Fatima and Our Lady of Lourdes packed the aisles and the porticoes of the side-doors. Black people who usually congregated on the bandstand opposite the Town Hall and Indians who sat on the railings around the statue of Mahatma Gandhi came too, pulled by this throng which had taken centuries to collect. Members of the Protestant community, business associates and the Freemasons took their places.

As four o'clock approached the Mother Superior of the convent of Cluny proceeded across the promenade with her community of nuns following, heads bowed beneath their fluttering linen veils.

Father Sebastian proceeded down the aisle in his capacious black satin cope, billowing out behind him, preceded by acolytes carrying holy water buckets, thuribles with burning coals for incense and candles. They took up their positions at the entrance of the church to receive the body of Cecile Monagas de los Macajuelos.

Father Sebastian had remembered the bells and he had ordered the sexton to begin tolling them at five minutes to four o'clock.

The clergy from the neighbouring parishes and the abbot of the monastery in the mountains filled the sanctuary. The church was dense with prayer and talcum powder.

The funeral, ancestral procession took years to battle through the traffic of the centuries and the streets. The people of the town waited for the cortege and the day to progress to the church and thence to Paradise Cemetery.

The procession was stuck in Cipero Street. The High Street was jammed. The orange sellers, the peanut and channa vendors at the library corner did a good trade with passengers hanging out of stationary taxis.

Gaston, the last descendant of the Monagas de los Macajuelos, who in these last days were famed for their still gargantuan statures, the mysterious circulation of their blood and the complexity of their digestive systems, had brought the town to a standstill. The projectors in the Radio City, the Rivoli, the Gaiety and the Globe flickered and went out over the matinee performances because no one could get to see them; Maureen O'Hara dying in the arms of Randolph Scott; the massacre of the North American Indians and the crimes of Chicago gangsters.

The people of the town of San Andres stood on the pavements and looked on at what was taking a long time to pass away. The bible preachers began their sermons of repentance between halleluias and the Baptist women lit their candles and rang their bell calling the people together. People were reminded to look at what was passing away and what was taking its place.

The funeral cortege sat in their misted up Mitsubishis, Toyotas, Mazdas, long American and chunky British limousines, refrigerated by air-conditioning.

At five minutes to four o'clock Father Sebastian sent an acolyte to give the sexton the signal to start with the tolling of the bells.

At each successive boom, the tolling of the funeral bells eventually penetrated the sunless and shuttered room at the back of Teresa's Hairdressing Salon. They eventually bored their way through the amnesiacal barrier into Gaston's memory. He suddenly remembered as he lay there, sweating, that this was the day that his grandmother had died and he was a pall bearer.

He leapt out of bed and picked up his pants from off the floor. He turned to the bed and said: 'Girl, ah go see yuh,' as he dashed out into the street pulling up his pants and buttoning his crutch.

The congested town heaved forward with the moving of Gaston's car.

It was already growing dark when the funeral procession eventually arrived at the church. Father Sebastian had buried the other dead. The Saint John Ambulance Brigade had attended to the fainting congregation.

The last obsequies were rushed so that Cecile could be buried before nightfall as the law stipulated.

The last shovel of earth was packed down on to the grave. Gaston's father patted him on the shoulder and said, 'Too much beti boy'.

Alicia, helped along with her one hundred years by Madoo, shook her head as she left the cemetery, 'So madam gone, eh Madoo, madam gone'.

THE GARDEN

Monica Furlong

Now that Flavia had been sent away Eleanora supposed that they would find her another orphan. She could imagine her now, bony, stubborn and painfully plain; her eyes would be lowered like a nun. Gradually she would put on weight, might even become pretty, but by then, Francesco or Ferdinando . . . It was, like so many other subjects, too depressing to think about.

In this, the last year of her life, the garden was the only thing she could bear to think about. Morning by morning she walked in the alleys, or rode in the pony-cart down the cypress avenue to the island and the tiny orange trees. There the horse Niccolo had sculpted rose from the lake with a rider on his back. She would feed the ducks, breathing orange scent. In the afternoons, when it was hot, she would sit with Flavia (before she was disgraced) in the summerhouse watching her favourite fountain. She was used to the fat cherubs whose feet hung over the basins, the grotesques with their pursed lips through which the water poured. So she shut out the thought of Cosimo and the children.

The garden was her creation – now the only one which still gave her pleasure. Nowadays, on the rare occasions when Cosimo came, it formed his only topic of conversation.

'Remarkable' he would say, looking about him, and only sometimes looking at her to try to detect the girl she had once been. 'An achievement.' Soon he would run out of things to say, and then, his duty done, he would go home, having noted her thinness, her sallow com-

[111]

plexion, how slowly she now walked. But she did not need, or want, Cosimo; just the garden.

Here, so many years ago now, she and Niccolo had drawn up the first plans for a sort of Paradise, tumbling down the hill from its wreath of statues above. There were three gardens really, each on a different level, with rose and yew hedges leading down through mysterious winding paths. In May the roses made a great web of flowers – you could walk through funnels coloured by their light. There was another garden with an ornate balustrade, from which you could lean out to view the river, its flight of bridges, and the domes of the city. There were cool avenues of trees down which peered fauns and satyrs, heroes and nymphs. She had given parties and masques in those green alleys and some of the revellers were now ghosts, but the marble people lived on.

There was a time when she knew every sculptor in the city and what he was capable of. She had haunted the workshops, looked at the uncut marbles, travelled to Carrara, talked of nymphs and *putti*, of Neptune, of the raped Sabines (how men loved that theme), and Mercury, of centaurs, sea monsters, artichokes and eagles.

In all of these plans she and Niccolo had worked together, in a ferment of enthusiasm, perpetually wanting to tell of the idea which had occurred late at night, or of the latest craftsman discovered. They had met almost daily, and even then had a boy running with messages between them. Her friendship with Niccolo had had a closeness she could not imagine with Cosimo, the father of her children. She remembered at their first meeting his long explanation of how it was almost impossible for there to be fountains in the proposed garden. Not expecting her interest and intelligence he had rattled off technical details about aquifers and water pressure. She listened, trying to set on one side the knowledge that in her lonely world she had found someone like herself, trying to ignore the way the wisdom in his face moved her. Finally she had said, faintly, 'Could you not build conduits from the river?'

'It would be very costly,' he had said.

'Quite so,' she had replied.

It was Niccolo who had thought of the name.

'What shall I call the garden?' she had said to him at one of their first meetings.

He scarcely knew her then, but looking at her in her golden prime, pregnant with Ferdinando, he had said 'Madam, Ceres is the queen and goddess who reigns here.' It was, of course, the comment of a courtier, yet she knew that he had seen into her deepest longing, to be rich and fruitful at her core instead of dry and sad. The next few years had been the nearest she had come. For Niccolo she learned to give up a little of the desperate selfishness she had learned as a child.

Later she had been disappointed at having yet another son (Cosimo was delighted, of course, but she had secretly hoped for a daughter). The birth had been as dreadful as the other, leaving her torn and angry, with the memory of being crazed from pain. She refused to look at the furious baby even while she fed him, yet she continued to feed him and did not find him a wet nurse. He was such a pretty baby that he charmed her in spite of herself – even as a baby Ferdinando had been irresistible.

Three years later Niccolo had died in a tavern brawl, some dispute over a boy they said. It crossed her mind that Cosimo had had him killed, jealous of him although he despised him. She had grieved for her friend for years. He had made his likeness for her in one of the Sileni on the fountain of the cherubs – ageless as time, wise, cruel, gentle, mysterious as the ancients. And she had called the garden after Ceres; had placed the fruitful goddess at the top of the topmost garden, symbol of what she, Eleanora, was not, but of what she worshipped.

Now twenty years later she knew that soon she would join Niccolo and other beloved friends. She calculated that she had one summer left to her, and that, as so often before, she would jealously watch the buds turn into flowers, and the flowers into fruit; day by day her garden, her art, would reveal her passion to her.

She was bitterly lonely. Her children, though they came dutifully to see her, were strangers. Her only real companion would be the orphan.

When, next morning, as she made her slow progress along the pleached walk, a pretty girl fell out of a tree at her feet, it simply did not occur to her that this could be the orphan, Cascia, though she was wearing the customary drab.

'There was a kitten stuck in the branches,' Cascia explained, sucking a clawed hand, and trying to rearrange her dress. 'Could you tell me how to find the Lady Eleanora? I'm to be her new maid.'

Seeing this girl with the bright brown eyes, the pretty bosom, the sunburned skin, Eleanora felt love. Before Cascia had risen from her curtsey, she had begun to plan a dress for her. Cascia's health and spirits were soon explained. (Nothing could explain beauty like hers.) She had spent only three chastening weeks being cared for by the sisters. Before that she had known the life of the farm, of a family of brothers and sisters. She struggled with tears as she told of the death of her parents in an epidemic, of the separation of the children. Eleanora tried to imagine such a happy family, such a grief, and could not quite do so, but she did her best to respond.

'Nothing can console you for such a loss' she said, 'but I hope you will be happy here.' The girl smiled at her through her tears and Eleanora's heart grew warmer. The girl was neither timid, nor silent – she was full of interest and curiosity over all the details of her new home. She asked about how the fountains worked, and about the stories of the figures on the statues. She drove the pony with the confidence of a farm girl. She seemed to know without being taught what Eleanora needed, when to give her her arm on the steps, to find her medicine. She brushed her hair, handed the pots for her make-up, washed her feet. Eleanora would not let her undress her, nor bathe her – she could scarcely bear to see herself undressed now and it was intolerable that the girl should do so.

'I see that you are ill, Madam,' the girl had said on their second day. 'I am used to nursing.' Eleanora was offended and did not reply. She was not ready to become an invalid.

There were many days on which she still felt well. Cascia sensed which they were, brought out her prettiest gowns that she had not worn for months, dressed her hair with jewels, coloured her cheeks. On the bad days (and there did not seem to be so many bad days since Cascia had come) she turned her face to the wall in despair. Cascia, to her surprise, stayed with her (her last maid had gone in search of the grooms), moving only to find a rose to place by her bedside, or, when she felt a little better, to bring a puppy to distract her. Cascia offered to massage her. Stiff and fearful at first, (it was many years now since anyone had touched her so intimately) Eleanora had eventually yielded herself to it, and to the soft husky sound of Cascia's singing. To

her astonishment the pain receded and she went to
sleep.

Another of Cascia's gifts was that of story-telling. She
did not tell stories of the gods and heroes – she was
unlettered and quite ignorant of such matters – but
slowly, perhaps to heal her own pain as much as to
amuse Eleanora, she began to talk at length about her
father and mother, about the farm, and about the life
Eleanora had never known and could scarcely imagine –
the life of the peasants.

'When we killed the pig' she would say, 'there was a
party. We were hungry because all through the summer
we fed the titbits to the pig, and then suddenly there was
enough to eat – we feasted like princes on pork dripping
with fat, and enough bacon and ham – all you could
hold. When everyone had had enough to eat and drink –
we drank our best wine with it – then we danced to
Rosco's violin . . .'

'My mother and I made cheeses – we had a wonderful
cow that year whose milk was yellow with cream . . .'

'My father and the men trapped hares. When I was
only six I learned to gut them. I was proud of the skill.
They made a fine stew . . .'

'My father gave me a linnet – it sang so sweetly – but I
left the door open and it flew away . . .'

'Livia married a boy from Siena. They are poor as
dirt or I would have lived with them, but they are very
happy. They love one another, you see, like my parents
did . . .'

'My father and mother were fourteen when they met.
They married the next year. I think my mother can no
longer have been a virgin because Giuseppe was born
six months later. Giuseppe went away to sea, you know,
and we never heard of him again. My mother grieved,
but hoped . . .'

[116]

Sometimes Cascia painted a picture of life in their cottage, and this was the part Eleanora liked best.

'The pig was in a pen underneath the house, you see – it smelled awful. Father had built shelves around the walls where we slept and we drew curtains across them to make beds. Sometimes I used to crawl into mine during the day and people would forget I was there, and my parents would say things they did not want the children to hear . . .' Cascia's brown eyes shone with mischief, but then the light went out of them.

'It was there that I learned of my father's illness . . .'

'At night my mother would put all the little ones to bed – she would sing to them and tell them stories, and kiss them many times – then she and my father and the big ones would eat their meal by candlelight, and the little ones would steal out of bed and want to sit on our laps or eat scraps and we would try to be stern but they were so pretty when they were naughty . . .' Again Cascia's eyes looked sad.

Eleanora tried to imagine this life. She compared it to the great palace at Toledo, to a childhood in which her grand, stiff clothes had compelled her to be still, to a mother she had rarely seen and could not remember being kissed by, and she was filled with envy.

'What . . . what is it like to be hungry?' she asked awkwardly at last. Cascia gave her a surprised glance.

'Sometimes it makes you very angry' she said, 'because when you long to eat and cannot do so then everything else in life is empty and hateful. But even then there are times when the hunger goes away and you go on with your life. When you eat, though, it is marvellous. The smell, the feel, the pleasure of the food in your mouth, of chewing and biting, with all your juices alive and flowing . . . perhaps it is worth being hungry sometimes.'

[117]

Eleanora had never had the experience she described.

'If your parents had not died' she said, changing the subject, 'what would have happened to you?'

'I should have married a local boy,' Cascia said simply.

'You had not already fallen in love as your parents did at fourteen?' Cascia flushed.

'It is no use to think of that,' she said. 'Those good times are past. There can be no dowry now.'

Eleanora was surprised to find that hours had passed as Cascia had talked, and that she herself was relaxed, interested in the life of another in a way that she had forgotten she could feel. She offered her supreme gift.

'May I tell you about my garden?' she asked.

In the days that followed the two of them talked incessantly, Cascia reliving her Tuscan childhood to Eleanora's fascinated audience, Eleanora describing the mechanics of the fountains, the different techniques of marble and of bronze, the importation of trees from distant parts of Europe, and the intricacies of grafting. Cascia listened with rapt interest, particularly when she talked of the great sculptors she had known.

'We were ignorant people,' she said once. 'We knew nothing of artists except sometimes a painter would come to work in the church or at the convent.' Although untutored, Cascia had a natural feeling for the sculpture, picking out the best pieces for admiration, ignoring the clumsy and the sentimental. Once, knowing Cosimo was away, Eleanora took her into the palace where she herself rarely went nowadays, to see the great pictures, the statues and candelabra. Cascia's eyes lit up with the wonder of it all and she spoke of the visit for days. On other good days Eleanora took her into the town to the churches where the best frescoes were to be found. Because of Cascia she had ceased to be a hermit, had found a new pleasure in living.

In the course of answering Cascia's questions she had found herself recounting legends and myths by the score – the Christian legends, and the classical legends that inspired her statues. It was something else she could give. In front of the huge crowned statue of Ceres she had told of Proserpine, the daughter stolen by Pluto, forced to spend six months of every year in the darkness of the underworld, but returning, bringing the spring flowers with her, to her loving mother. Cascia listened thoughtfully to this tale.

'Poor Proserpine. Poor Ceres,' she said. 'But they had something to look forward to. It could have been worse.'

Ferdinando came one afternoon as they were sitting sleepily in the summerhouse lulled by the fretted music of the fountains.

'Mother, you are looking better,' he said. Eleanora knew that she had some colour in her yellow cheeks from the pleasure of her life with Cascia, that her hair had been becomingly dressed by Cascia that morning, that she was wearing a gown of a rich blue that Cascia had discovered, unworn, in her closet. She inclined her head. She saw his eyes travel to Cascia and move from face to breasts to buttocks with that calculating male glance. A faint dread stirred in her.

As the two of them walked alone in the garden he asked about her, and listened gravely while she told the child's story.

'She is not for you, Ferdinando,' she finished. 'She is a child. A virgin.'

He changed the subject and asked the name of a flower that fell cascading through the branches of the trees – he had always known how to charm her. But the calculation was still in his glance when they rejoined Cascia.

'He's nice,' said Cascia, when he had gone.

'He's a spoiled child,' said Eleanora, but then paused. It was true that Ferdinando was an indulged son of his father, yet he was spoiled in another sense. Cosimo had taken him from her when he was little more than a baby, her darling, her favourite. He had picked him up in his arms one day, without warning, carrying him away to make him into a man, his fat little legs kicking, his voice pitifully crying 'Mama, mama . . .' For this she had never forgiven Cosimo, but he had had his way. He had made a man of Ferdinando, separated him from the taint of women. And now Ferdinando sought it compulsively as others sought wine.

The roses were glorious that year, perhaps the best they had ever been, rivers of red and white tumbling from tree and basin and balcony, spilling their scent in the air. Once she made a crown of roses for Cascia, carefully removing the thorns.

'There!' she said, 'I crown you Queen of the Summer!' The flowers reflected in Cascia's shining black hair, and her eyes too shone with the love that Eleanora gave her. For a moment Eleanora saw not her substitute daughter, Cascia, but a moment of eternity, a crack in the fabric of things that gave her this astonishing vision. Then she knew what Niccolo had seen in his boys and ceased to be jealous.

'Madam, I have something to ask you,' said Cascia timidly. 'You will tell me if it is a liberty, but I wondered . . . Could you teach me to read? You see, I never had the chance.'

Suddenly removed from her mystical vision of Cascia, Eleanora was still delighted. Now weak, dying, in-

creasingly dependent on Cascia for the labour of getting
up, or moving about, or being soothed in her pain, there
was yet another gift she could offer. Cascia made her rich.

Four weeks later, weeks in which the pain had
suddenly taken a giant stride forward (although in its
intervals she and Cascia had struggled laboriously over
letters and words) Cascia had another request.

'In my village, Madam, there is a wise woman, Mad-
dalena, who knows about stilling pain. I could go to see
her, get some herbs from her . . . It would make it
easier for you . . .'

Eleanora hesitated. She dreaded the loss of the girl
for even a few days – her life revolved around her now as
hitherto it had revolved around the garden, yet the pain
had frightened her very much. She had moved near to
the boundary at which all dignity is lost, at which she
might be reduced to the sobbing shame of a prisoner in
the hands of a torturer. (She had heard those voices
often enough in the distance when she lived with Cosimo.) For her own sake, and for Cascia's, she must find
an alternative. At the beginning, before Cascia had
come, she had planned suicide, had secreted a poison in
a vase in her room. Cascia had come across it one day
when she was arranging her things – a good day . . .

'Do you want this, Madam?' she had enquired
matter-of-factly, knowing well what it was, and Eleanora had replied, 'No, no, I don't want that. Throw it
away.'

'You will take the carriage' she said now, 'and Primo
shall drive you.'

Another child came to take Cascia's place, and Eleanora
groaned at her stupidity and her slowness. The four
days seemed interminable; she planned another dress
for Cascia, Cascia who had never worn silk in her life.

[121]

Also she pondered, with the meditation of a lover, on all the stories Cascia had told her of her life; the farm, the children, the parents, the neighbours, passed before her like a series of frescoes. She drew energy from them. She compared them with her own memories, memories in which it was always winter and always cold, though she knew that she had ever complained of the heat beneath her stifling clothes. No one had touched her except the dwarf Runi, who used to push her on her swing when she was five; the two of them were the same height.

Then her father had exchanged her as he might exchange a beautiful painting, a fine horse; still only half grown-up she had left her native country and become Cosimo's wife. Always she had thought, 'Soon life will start and I will be happy.' But what had happened had been Cosimo's brutal love-making, the weary months of pregnancy, and the horror of childbirth.

She sent the substitute maid away so that Cascia's arrival would not be spoiled, and sat by Niccolo's fountain to wait. The first stars came out. As if bred by the memory of her childhood, bitter thoughts began to grow in her mind. Perhaps Cascia would come late to torture her. Perhaps indeed she would not come at all, but take this chance to escape from her bondage. Perhaps she was on her way back in the carriage weeping at the thought of her return. It grew so late that Eleanora went in and lay on her bed, turning her face to the wall in longing, beginning to weep.

But then she could hear running feet in the garden, the door of the summerhouse burst open and there was Cascia, her eyes alight with joy, talking, talking, at the speed at which only Cascia could talk.

'The carriage got its wheels stuck in the mud and both Primo and I had to get down and put our shoulders to it.

Primo was furious – he was wearing his best coat . . .
Oh, it was lovely meeting everybody again. My youngest brother is so well taken care of – the innkeeper's wife
took him, you know, she could not have children of her
own – he's quite fat – and she gave me some of her own
sausage to bring back for you to taste. Maria sent you
some of her cheese – I think it's the best in Tuscany – oh
yes, and there's some ham. Lucrezia gave me a loaf.
Ruffino gave me some wine – I have longed for the taste
of the wine we had in the village. And herbs – I've
brought back lots of nice ones for your omelettes – and
my eldest brother, who is working with the blacksmith
now, sent you this decoration he had made. I told him
about Ceres . . .'

Cascia held up a device of ears of corn wrought in
metal. Her gaze fell upon Eleanora's wasted face.

'Dear Madam, I have missed you,' she said, and then
naturally, without presumption, she put her arms
round Eleanora and kissed her on the cheek. They
feasted upon all the treasures Cascia had brought back
with her. It seemed to Eleanora, as she ate the strong
ham and drank the rough wine, that she had entered
Cascia's former life as through a sacrament, that its
grace was pouring into her.

'Lucca?' she enquired. Cascia blushed once more.

'He is not promised to anyone. We talked. It's no
good, of course. I told him that.' She changed the
subject quickly, prattling on about the journey.

'The pain-killer?' Eleanora asked at last, unwillingly.
Cascia drew out two flasks, one big and full of a green
liquid, the other tiny and black.

'A few drops of this in water when you are in pain will
ease you,' she said. 'When the pain gets worse we just
increase the quantity.'

'And the other?'

[123]

'When the green liquid no longer works – and it will for a long time – then you may wish to . . . go more quickly. It must be drunk all at once and will work fast.' As she told her this Cascia held her hand, looking compassionately into her face.

'Good,' said Eleanora. 'Let us put it away for now. I do not wish to see it again until I need it.'

She slept well that night, with the scent of Tuscan herbs in her nostrils. When it was time to wash and dress next morning she did not send Cascia away.

'I want you to see me as I am,' she said, hot with shame at what the disease had done to her white, shapely body. Cascia looked gravely, without recoil, at the monstrous thing that had happened to her – Eleanora would have noticed if she had flinched.

'I see,' she said. 'Now I can bathe you.'

And she did so with her strong, gentle touch. Eleanora felt that now her ultimate secret had been shown she could relax. As if relaxing had loosened her tongue she began to talk almost as freely as Cascia herself – of her cold and lonely childhood, of her early marriage, of her homesickness for Spain. She tried to be loyal to Cosimo and to her sons, but the pitiful glance that Cascia turned upon her showed her that the girl had guessed what she had not said.

'Men,' said the girl, 'they puzzle me.'

'They live like conquerors,' said Eleanora.

'*All* men?' asked Cascia.

Eleanora remembered a secretary who had comforted her as Cosimo's lonely, terrified bride – a slender young man from the south – who had bedded her gently until Cosimo . . .

'No, not all men,' she said.

'In the village' Cascia said once, 'we used to imagine

[124]

what it would be like to be a princess – to wear silk and cloth of gold and jewels, always to have enough to eat, not to be worked to death . . . Then it seemed wonderful.' She paused. 'Yet it is terrible to be poor, to fear to starve, to be in debt . . .'

High summer reached its peak. The intensity of green was like a pressure – as if Nature was staring at one from too close a range. The flowers shone like lamps all over the garden, thrusting, and bursting and tumbling, in purple and yellow and orange. The heat stood implacably over everything. Soon, Eleanora knew, all would be baked and brown, dead before winter came on – she dreaded that summer desert.

She was much weaker now, moving only from the summerhouse to the little garden with the fountains. Her thinness made her wretchedly uncomfortable, waking her with the pain of lying on her own bones in bed, tormenting her as she sat in her chair. Cascia slept beside her now, getting up to turn her, or make her a drink. Sometimes in the early hours of the morning they ate little feasts or laughed together, like two children awake when they should be asleep, delighting in their own wit, the fun of being together.

Eleanora's sons had taken to coming with great regularity. Nearly every afternoon brought one of them.

'They must love you,' said Cascia, but with interrogation in her voice.

'I have possessions,' Eleanora explained wearily. 'Farms, houses, a castle in Umbria . . .'

'But they are rich men, are they not?' said Cascia in wonder. 'Why should they crave for more?'

'Riches are like wine. The taste grows with habit. None are so greedy as the rich.'

Ferdinando stared at Cascia. It was not only riches he

wished to take from his mother. In one sleepless night while Cascia, exhausted, dozed beside her, Eleanora brooded. If Ferdinando ravished Cascia, as he had Flavia, if her baby was then taken from her to be brought up in the orphanage, if Cascia herself, dishonoured, was reduced to servitude or begging, Cascia's fate was the lot of women. They were disposable. Eleanora's loyalty was owed to Cosimo and her sons. She could send Cascia away, of course, before Ferdinando trapped her – she could give her a dowry and her dresses, ask Primo to drive her home once more, employ another orphan. Eleanora groaned. All her life she had feared to die alone.

Cascia woke immediately and found the green flask.

The next afternoon Cascia came in from a walk in the garden alert but troubled. Eleanora, who knew all her moods, tried to read this one. Within the hour Ferdinando arrived, giving Cascia a glance of complicity.

'My son met you in the garden this afternoon?' Eleanora asked later, blushing as if the shame were hers.

'Yes.'

'What then?'

Cascia did not reply but looked fully at Eleanora with troubled eyes.

'Shall I guess? He kissed you, and then he made a suggestion. That the two of you should lie together in one of the summerhouses.'

Cascia still did not answer, so Eleanora went on. 'You think that I am disloyal to my son? That I speak of what a mother should not speak of? Or you think that I am jealous?'

'No.' Cascia's voice was huskier than usual. 'I do not think you are jealous. He did kiss me. He did . . . make a suggestion. I did not comply.' The brown eyes looked at Eleanora.

'I must tell you – I wanted to. He is so fine, there is

such a sweetness in him, how could anyone resist? It is nothing to do with virtue or sense.'

'But yet you didn't?'

'Only because you were waiting for me and I might be found out.'

'Oh Cascia!'

That night they lay silent in the darkness, both of them awake. Once, towards morning, Cascia said doubtfully, 'I could promise you that I will not . . .'

Eleanora did not answer.

In the morning she was strong, fierce.

'I wish to go out today,' she told Cascia. 'One last look at my garden before I take to my bed. Ask Primo to harness the pony-cart, but you shall drive it.'

In the early morning cool they saw as much of the garden as you could see from the pony-cart. They drove down the cypress avenue, they looked at the horse rising from the lake and picked an orange from the rows of orange trees on the island. They watched fountains play, and they visited statues of long-dead heroes. From afar they looked at the great statue of Ceres with the gardens hanging before her – she was only to be reached by those who could climb. They moved through sunshine and leafy shadow.

'Here,' said Eleanora suddenly. 'Leave the cart here. I wish to walk.' Surprised, Cascia helped her down from the cart and gave her her stick. But she leaned heavily and Cascia hoped they would not walk far. In the middle of a walk was a tiny temple, with a statue of Proserpine fleeing in terror in the middle of it. In front of it stood a fountain with its bank of nymphs and cherubs and behind it stood the usual little door through which the gardener went to clear pipes and check pressure. Eleanora pulled at a chain round her

neck and produced a key with which she unfastened the
door. It opened into the rocky chamber that led to the
fountains, but there was another door which Eleanora
also unlocked. Beyond it was a narrow tunnel leading
away into the darkness.

Having shown Cascia this Eleanora drew the girl back
into the garden, locking both doors again, and made her
painful way back to the pony-cart.

Cascia was curious.

'Where does the tunnel lead?'

'Niccolo made it for me many years ago,' said Eleanora. 'In those days I longed to see the world, to know the
things that I could never know as Cosimo's wife. Niccolo, who loved disguises, suggested a tunnel through
which I could pass when I needed to escape. The tunnel
comes out in a garden Niccolo once owned near the
river. He would meet me there with boy's clothes and
together we would explore taverns and theatres, we
would go to carnivals and festivals.' Her voice was glad
at the memory of her friendship with Niccolo.

'It seemed to me that you may need it for a different
purpose.' She spoke deliberately, a princess who was
used to having her own way. 'I shall write a letter to my
greatest living friend, Angelo of Siena (he lives now in
the town here – he is treasurer to Cosimo), and tell him
to help you back to your village and to see that you
marry Lucca. Whether or not you are . . . There are
ways of making it seem . . .' Her voice cracked with pain,
with jealousy, with shame for her son. 'You think you do
not love Lucca now but once you are away it will be different.
Yes, I will see that there is a dowry . . . But remember,
Cascia, I rely on you to escape. That I ask you to promise.'

Cascia had listened to all of this with wide, slightly
frightened eyes.

'Madam, I hate caves and tunnels . . . the dark.'

[128]

'We all have to learn to go through the dark, to squeeze our way through. I will go into my dark and you into yours.' Now her voice was harsh.

At night they lay silent, both of them awake. Eleanora groaned, not with the pain of her body but with the pain of her mind, and immediately Cascia got up and lit the lamp to pour the medicine. Eleanora drank it with a sort of contempt.

'Now you hate me,' Cascia said, her eyes pleading.

'You let them divide us,' said Eleanora. They looked at each other, one a princess, the other a peasant, two conquered people.

'Does my . . . love . . . for Ferdinando mean that I no longer love you?'

Eleanora saw how in her poverty she needed Cascia's love so badly. She remembered another's eyes – Niccolo's – when he had first told her about himself, and saw that the best thing she had done was to give him his freedom.

She took Cascia in her arms and kissed her.

'Do what you must but *get away*,' she said. 'As soon as I am dead, without waiting.'

The heat wore on and the earth of the garden was cracked and powdery. Movement was difficult for Eleanora now. Cascia tended her as lovingly as ever, only in the afternoons when Eleanora was supposed to sleep, she left, quiet as a shadow. On one such afternoon Eleanora sat by Niccolo's fountain and thought with passion of Niccolo and Cascia. By a miracle they had come to her and made her rich. Each had disappointed her but perhaps that did not matter; it had exercised the love in her, strengthened it until it could throw away the crutch of selfishness and stand alone. Yet now there was one more painful exercise, one in which she had counted on Cascia's warm presence and her strong brown hand. She fought with her selfishness once more and defeated it. She took the black liquid and returned to her bed.

She wept for loneliness, as much for the child in Toledo as for Cosimo's wife. She groaned in fear of the dark, of the pain to come. She knew that it would be another couple of hours before Cascia returned and long before then . . .

She drifted, tossing on the waves of the drug, searching, frightened. In a kind of dream she believed she had wandered out of the palace at Toledo and found her way to the slums she had often passed in her carriage where the dirty children had stared. She was lost, all unskilled as she was in the ways of the world. She wandered down endless alleyways, full of people staring. She was the only one who moved. There was something to be afraid of, only she could not remember what it was. Was she in danger, and if so, why?

'Madam, I will help you,' said Cascia's voice, and Eleanora told herself in the dream that she was dreaming, but then she could feel her fingers firmly held.

'I'm so frightened,' she said pitifully.

'It's all right. I had a feeling you might need me. I'm here and will stay with you. It won't be long and it will be so easy, so easy . . .'

'You will go? Afterwards?'

'I will go. Just as you said. To marry Lucca.'

It seemed to Eleanora that the person who asked the question and the person who answered it were one and the same, that Cascia's life was also her life and Cascia's happiness her happiness. She smiled.

So it was that both women went into the dark together.

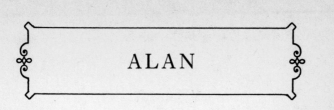

ALAN

Peter Benson

Alan was an exceptional ten-year-old. He had worked things out, and with the help of a chemistry set, learnt that life had boundaries, drawn to protect reality. Equations, Formulae. Meaning. For example: he put some mercuric oxide (HgO) in a test tube, heated it, and waited for a silvered sheen to appear on the glass. Then he took a glowing splint and put it in the tube. It was rekindled. He smiled. Oxygen was given off by the heated oxide. Oxygen was always given off by the heated oxide. Antoine Lavoisier (1743–1794) had done the same trick as he conducted his famous combustion experiments. Lavoisier was one of Alan's heroes. A clever Frenchman who knew tax collectors. These people had helped the great scientist escape the guillotine.

Mercuric oxide, like any of the other oxides, hydroxides, carbonates, bicarbonates, sulphides, nitrates etc, following rules so exact they were beautiful to Alan, as he bent over his conical flasks and racks of test-tubes. He didn't want to do the normal boy's things, and would have been happy to stay in his room all the time. Climbing trees, riding bikes or kicking heels in the street wasn't his idea of fun, as he scribbled $2Hg0 > 2Hg + 0_2$ absent-mindedly.

Absent-mindedly because it was Wednesday, and his reveries were interrupted by his mother. She opened his door and stood there. He hated that. Why didn't she knock? He had to knock before going in her room. Why wasn't he afforded the same courtesy? Rules should be consistent – he thought, as she opened her mouth and said 'Come on Alan! It's not that bad. You know when I was your age, I learnt to play the piano too. It did me good!'

Good?

'I' she continued, 'went to a woman called Mrs Hurd. She used to cook spaghetti and feed starlings with it, but only because she missed Italy. She'd played in the opera house in Milan, and wanted to remind herself of the great days.'

Alan nodded. 'I know,' he said. He'd heard the story so many times it was boring. Why couldn't she understand that he wasn't interested in music? Why couldn't she see? Why did she have a nervous facial tic that irritated him so much? Why did she think playing the piano would improve him? He wanted understanding for what he was, or something like that.

But he went anyway. His teacher was called Miss Maxwell. He was taken in the car, the seats were uncomfortable, and it was raining.

'It always rains on Wednesday,' he said.

'No it doesn't,' said his mother, and changed gear. 'That's a silly thing to say. It didn't last week.'

'Well it felt like it.'

Mother grimaced. 'What do you mean, felt like it?' Sometimes, the odd places her son's mind wandered into made her worry. 'It can't feel like it's raining if it's not.'

'Yes it can,' Alan said, and meant it.

'Alan! Now you're being silly.' She'd forgotten how to give him a decent telling-off. Not that she'd ever known really. The boy was an only child, and indulged rather.

'You said I was silly before.'

'I didn't!'

'Yes you did. You said that saying it always rained on Wednesday was a silly thing to say.'

'Alan?'

'Yes?'

His mother indicated, changed down, braked and said, 'Look! We're here.'

Here. Here was Miss Maxwell's house. It was a Victorian 'Villa' though everyone knew that was a stupid affectation. The only real villas were built by the Romans. Perfectly proportioned, white walls, togas – the Victorians had built fat grey houses that looked wet even in summer. People – thought Alan – should call things what they were.

Miss Maxwell's villa was a very brooding example of the type. It rose three stories to a tiny attic window, built in a terrace of similar houses in the rain.

Limp net curtains protected Miss Maxwell's rooms from the outside having a peer in; a heavy door with no window waited for their knock.

Alan said, 'Why's it called a villa when it's not?'

'But it is. The people that built houses like this had every right to call it one.' She knocked on the door.

'They didn't.'

Alan's mother looked at him. She thought about saying something sharp, but didn't have the heart. The boy would have to sort himself out. She was past it, she decided.

The knock had alerted Miss Maxwell's dogs. They barked. Alan thought 'Oh God,' and waited as his mother wished her son would say 'Why?' and really want an answer. But he always answered his own questions. He never failed. He was a strange boy. As the chain was drawn out of its catch, the latch turned and the door opened.

Miss Maxwell said, 'Heel!' to her dogs – spaniels – who jumped up and licked Alan's face.

'Ugh,' he went, and backed off. He hated dogs. He

didn't like them always wanting affection, staring with doleful eyes. They couldn't be relied upon to do what you expected. Nor could Miss Maxwell, but he didn't know that then. He just thought she was a stupid Scottish woman who didn't have enough money to go home to Scotland where she belonged.

'Here we are!' said his mother. The dogs were being dragged away. They smelt of their rotten ears.

'Come in! You'll get soaked standing there! And the wee laddie!' Miss Maxwell had a loud voice. She smiled. Alan hated being called a wee laddie more than anything. He could almost kill Miss Maxwell for it. And in front of his mother. He was nearly eleven (in four months) and that wasn't far off twelve which was as good as thirteen. And once you were in your teens you could do anything. He knew that, and couldn't wait. No more piano lessons then, no more wee laddie. Science would overcome.

His mother left. She'd be back in an hour. She had some shopping to do. A frozen chicken, some socks, a tin of magnolia paint. She smiled at Miss Maxwell and told Alan to play nicely. 'He's been practising,' she said.

'Good,' said Maxwell, and led the way down a dank smelling corridor to the music room, where the piano sat in frosty silence surrounded by piles of music, the remains of old meals and a single moose head, hanging at a slant on the wall between photographs of trees and log cabins in Canada.

The story of how Miss Maxwell came to have a moose head is long and complicated – boring even – something hardly worth the bother of telling here. It's enough to say that Miss Maxwell's brother – Malcolm Maxwell – had lived the greater part of his life in the Yukon, chasing Klondike gold and cheap whisky. The moose

head had been won in a bet and survived two decades of
harsh living before coming to England in a box that was
sister to the box Malcolm Maxwell lay in. Like a warning, that head, with its fat glass eyes and moth-eaten old
chin. Miss Maxwell was used to it now, and enjoyed its
company. An echo of the Maxwells' influence around
the world; she said, 'In you go,' to Alan, and made
herself comfortable in her listening chair.

Alan sat at the piano. The fire wasn't lit. The room
was cold. He couldn't reach the pedals. Miss Maxwell
offered to lower the seat for him.

'Yes please.'

She stood up and took hold of the knobs that screwed
it down. He felt her dress rub against him, and her
smell. She smelt of talcum powder and cloves, and he
shivered. He didn't like being that close to people. He
concentrated on the thought of a test-tube of copper
sulphate. Something with a glassy smell – it helped him
ignore the woman's horrible breath, and a whispered,
'Better?' in his ear. He nodded. He wanted to say 'Let's
just get it over with,' but daren't. He might have
thought she was a stupid woman, but he was still a little
afraid of her. There was something about her curly
mouth and the blood-vessels showing beneath her
cheeks. Thousands of tiny scarlet cobwebs. She had
grey hair too, and was old. How old, he couldn't guess,
but old enough, he thought. But not too old not to
have forgotten how to give him lip if he gave her lip,
so when she said, 'Show me what you've been practising. The Minuet, wasn't it?' he shrugged and began
to play.

He might have loathed music, but he had a light
touch, and played the piece well. His phrasing was
expressive, the notes were given colour. Lights and
darks. His talent belied his feelings, and when he fin-

ished Miss Maxwell patted him on the back and said,
'Well done. You have been practising.'

'A bit.' A bit, but only because his mother bothered
him if he didn't.

'More than a bit, I'd say. It was very good. You've got
a real talent, Alan.'

'Have I?'

Miss Maxwell wasn't surprised. Any other pupil
would have been pleased to be told they had talent, but
Alan wasn't any other pupil. He was her odd one, the
one who didn't like the lessons, and didn't know what
serious application could achieve. He was wasting talent
but not knowing he had it. Why?

'You don't seem very pleased,' she said.

'No,' he said, meaning 'why should I be?' But he
wouldn't say that. He wanted the lesson to finish but
didn't want trouble. It was bad enough just sitting
there, the Canadian photographs fading, the atmosphere
in the room like one on a foggy moor, the rain falling.

'You're just being modest,' Miss Maxwell said, and
she wondered if that was all he was being. It couldn't be.

The moose looked down as she ruffled his hair. He
hated that. 'Play the Polonaise now.'

The Polonaise was in the key of F, by J. S. Bach.
Number five in a book of selected pieces from his 'Little
notebook for Anna Magdalena,' it was a sweet tune, and
Alan concentrated. He stuck exactly to the time, the
finger-marks and the marked phrasing.

The moose was baleful. Its ears couldn't hear a thing.
It didn't smell of Canada any more, and the dogs lay on
the floor beneath it. They made irritating snuffling
sounds as he played the music.

Plink, plonk, pedal, plonk . . . He struggled with the
left hand in the section after the last repeat, but successfully, and turned the corner into the last eight bars with

confidence. For a moment, he almost enjoyed himself in that room with his breath steaming and the moose looking down. Some of the Canadian photographs had brown watermarks where mountains and trees had once been, one of the piano keys stuck. He was annoyed with it. Something fouling the rules; he shook his head and went back to concentrating on the Polonaise.

The sound of the rain accompanied his playing, the gloom of the room was the audience. Silent Miss Maxwell was the conductor. She was very quiet as he played, chilled by the music.

He let the notes get into his head and tickle his mind with their order. He was very strict with himself over order. Everything needed it, and the piece would have been nothing but a jumble without it. With it it meant something – though not as much as the simplest of chemical formulae. H_2O say – as he finished with a small flourish, put his hands on his knees and turned to look at Miss Maxwell.

He'd never seen a dead person before, but from pictures and the television he thought he had a good idea. And Miss Maxwell looked like she had the idea.

She was very still, and her face had changed colour from its flushed pink to grey. Her eyes were closed, her mouth was hanging open. No sound came from her body, and from where he sat he couldn't see her move at all. One arm rested on her lap, the other hung over the side of the chair, the hands limp and not tapping time any more. Only the sound of the dogs snoring disturbed the freezing air.

For a moment he didn't move. He wasn't going any closer to Miss Maxwell than he was already. He knew she was dead and that was that. He wasn't going to check for a pulse. His instincts told him he should. Theories about things had to be proved with facts; but when he looked at her face it was more obvious than the most blatant fact. She was dead.

He watched the rain streak the window, and he ignored the moose. It had seen death before, and wasn't impressed. It moulted a bit, and echoed the silence in its glass eyes.

Any other ten-year-old, finding himself in a dank house with a dead body and a silent piano would have pissed with fright, but Alan didn't. He was shocked by Miss Maxwell's death, confused even, but he applied logic. Death was what came for everyone, like it came to animals, like it had come for the hamster he'd once kept. A fat and boring rodent that only came out at night, and then only to trundle a wheel; he hadn't been upset by its death. He'd shrugged then as he shrugged now in Miss Maxwell's direction.

He looked at his watch. His mother would collect him in ten minutes. All he could do was wait. He couldn't get hold of the police or an ambulance. Miss Maxwell hadn't got a phone. By the time he got to a phone box he'd be wet and his mother would have missed him and found the body and panicked and then things would be worse than they were already.

'So,' he said to the piano. 'That's it.' He closed Anna Magdalena's little notebook, stood up, and thought about the cup of drinking-chocolate Miss Maxwell always made him at the end of the lesson. She'd never make another one, but that didn't stop him thinking that he'd make one himself.

So he went to the kitchen. The dogs didn't leave their spot on the floor. They hadn't noticed their mistress's condition, or maybe, Alan thought, they're dead too. But they weren't. They watched him leave the room with half-open eyes, and hadn't sensed anything odd, other than the fact that he'd stopped playing ten minutes too soon. They were stupid dogs, but had a good sense of time. Time, sleep, sleep, time, bone, biscuit, short walk, tree, piss, bone, time, sleep, sleep. It was a dog's life.

Alan walked down the corridor to the kitchen. It was dark, an old oil-painting of a woman in a frilled bonnet hung in the gloom. The woman's eyes were dull but had been painted with a flourish, and shone at their corners. They didn't wink but they could have in that gloomy corridor as he walked beneath them, opened the kitchen door, smelt the must and thought, 'Hot drinking-chocolate.'

He'd stood in that kitchen and watched Miss Maxwell make hot chocolate many times, but when he tried to remember where the tin was he couldn't. It wasn't on any shelves, so he switched the light on and began to open cupboards.

He found the dog food, some bottles of disinfectant, and a half empty bottle of whisky marked 'Saturdays only.' He found a bag of potatoes and some gooseberries in a covered bowl, and was about to forget about the drink and just sit down to wait for his mother when he found the tin. It was behind some packets of tea, so he took it out, found a mug and boiled a kettle. Enough water for one cup – no one else in the house would be having one.

He drank as the dirty afternoon wore on and the sky darkened. February was a dreadful month, he thought, as he sipped and watched the rain fall. He wasn't spooked by the thought of a dead body sitting in the other room, but as the darkness gloomed around him he did shiver once, though from cold, not fright. He was a stable boy, thinking about the realities of life as he sat there. He wasn't interested in the sort of worries other children had. Ones about ghosts and monster people with dripping skin coming back to life. He didn't imagine that he was in danger, and sipped again.

A car passed the house, spraying the pavement with water. It didn't stop. It wasn't his mother. He looked at his watch again. Five minutes to go.

His father had given him the watch. It had been a present from New York. His father had been to a meeting there. It wasn't the sort he'd wanted – one with a built-in calculator and a button for time zones – but it had a stop-watch feature and a light, so it wasn't bad. He counted the seconds as they flashed by, anticipating each number before it came, pleased by the regular way the digits were built from the little black dashes.

As the drinking-chocolate cooled, he took bigger gulps and stared at the single light. It didn't hurt his eyes. Miss Maxwell only used forty-watt bulbs. He wondered why. They were hardly an economy, especially when you strained your eyes because they weren't bright enough. And they cast such a cold light as he heard a thump, somewhere in the house, when he wasn't expecting a thump at all. He jolted in his seat, tilted his head to listen for another, put his cup down and was about to stand up when he remembered. The dogs. One of them had bumped into something, or knocked something off a shelf. They were always doing things like that. Breaking china or disturbing furniture. Miss Maxwell had often complained about them, loving them all the same, but shaking her head at them.

With her dead what would happen to the dogs? Alan wondered about that. They were too old and disgusting to appeal to new owners. Too blind and smelly. If someone wanted a dog they'd buy a puppy. Something bouncy and cute. Like a baby, thought Alan. And with Miss Maxwell stiff, her dogs would end up stiff too, he decided. He'd seen something on the television about the number of dogs put down every year by the RSPCA. Miss Maxwell's would join that number. They wouldn't be knocking into furniture for much longer.

He finished the chocolate. His mother was late. She often was. She often got talking at the shops about ways to cook things, or how the weather had been so awful.

So Alan cursed her as he rinsed his mug and watched the rain teem on. He couldn't even sit on the garden wall to wait for her. As it was there'd be a terrible fuss when she arrived. Dead Miss Maxwell would have to be seen to. Policemen would be fetched and he thought it was a safe bet that he'd have to talk to them. They'd want to know he hadn't murdered her (how often he'd thought he'd like to) and they'd maybe even take him down the station. He'd seen that on the television too. Flashing lights, sirens, detectives asking, 'this the body?' when it was obvious. And, 'this the boy?' when he'd be the only boy in the room. The least he could do was gather up his music.

He switched the kitchen light off and walked down the corridor to the music-room. It was darker than when he'd walked the other way, and a gust of wind rattled the front door. A tangy smell clung to the walls, and the faces of the people in the pictures that hung there were sightless as he opened the music-room door and disturbed the dogs.

Miss Maxwell was sitting as he'd left her, one arm resting on her lap, the other hanging down by her side. Her face was as grey as it had been, her skin slack, her eyes shut. Alan kicked the side of the piano. Its strings echoed from what seemed miles away, one of the dogs sat up, Alan winced, Miss Maxwell opened her eyes, blinked and said, 'Oh Alan! I'm sorry. Did I drop off?'

Alan felt his spine crease and twist along its length, and a sensation unlike anything he'd ever experienced swept into his stomach. His bladder let go as everything he thought he believed in crumbled around him. Things following rules. People staying dead when they were. The stuffed head of a moose moulting in a damp atmosphere.

Alan heard Miss Maxwell. She was saying, 'Are you quite well laddie? You look like death warmed up!' but the words jangled in his head as he dropped Anna Magdalena's little notebook and the sound of falling rain was crumpled by the sound of his mother's car.

NO MARKS
FOR ROLF

Sue Krisman

Rolf Klausen had set down neat piles of yesterday's paper, the thick *Stuttgarterzeitung*, ideal for soaking up any dampness from the morning's rain. He was unfolding and shaking out the black plastic sheet to cover them when the motorcycle approached, hesitated, then stopped beside him officiously.

He tutted and sighed. A 'move on' so soon. He should have known. That such a dry railway arch, covered in with so elegant a piece of ironwork might be unlived in, had been too good to hope for. Never mind, further into the centre of Stuttgart, he'd maybe find even a better place. And nearer to the Liederhall for later.

Rolf let the plastic fall where it fell and looked up to wait placidly for the city rules to be quoted at him. The by-laws of 1951, it might be. Or Ancient City Ordinances. Sometimes it was both.

Or it might be 'social services available for the destitute'. Even 'police cells if you've not moved on by night-fall'. He'd heard them all. Threats and kindness. Here it came. The identity card. The town-hall had given this motor-cyclist boy an enormous prime number to be registered by, Rolf noticed, memorizing it before handing the numbered card back.

'—Stuttgart is proud to welcome you if you are new here,' the young man was saying in a flat voice. 'Please try not to leave litter in this handsome city. In this leaflet are a list of addresses that you may use as hostels but even if you prefer not to go there, Stuttgart Council ask you to accept this for your comfort and well-being.

I, or one of my colleagues, will bring the same amount
to you each day.'

Rolf stared at the two limp green five-mark notes in
the boy's hand and shook his head, making no move to
take either the money or the leaflet from the boy's other
hand. Turning away he started to organize and unpack.
Incredibly, he had permission to stay in this fine spot.
There were things to do.

Not two minutes before, he had passed a rubbish tip.
Tips meant mattresses. Saucepans, sometimes. And
look at those steps. Up and over to the station. Railway
timetables had wonderful numbers in them. Stations
had water and toilets. Timetables; he could add the
numbers, cube them, square them, fractionalize them,
factorize them, take an average of the time to journey
north and compare it with the journeys . . .

The young man stood there, the notes still in his
hand, annoyance hardening in his face. 'Stuttgart are
proud of this new idea. Every day we bring you ten
marks. Every day you can eat well and look after yourself, then when you're – er – strong again you'll look for
work and move into your own home and pay taxes and
Stuttgart will give your taxes to help other – homeless
people until one day we don't have any more tramps. *Gut?*'

Rolf clapped his hands over his head in delight and
smiled, shaking his head and turning back to his packs,
untying the difficult knots that held in place the little
three-legged stove he'd found in the Frankfurt tip.
When your stove stood sentry at the front of your patch,
your bundles were safe, even if you weren't there.
Casual travellers might rob you while you slept, kill
you, even, but a stove was a tramp's front door and no
man of the road would touch so much as a winter sock if
a stove were there. He set it up, propped the third leg
with half a slate so that it stood steady and . . .

'You. You take ten marks,' the boy shouted, tact and training draining away in his uneasiness. 'They are to help you, can you hear? I have to give them to you. Not for drink, I have to say, but who listens. Look . . .'

Rolf snatched them without looking up, stuffed them into his coat-sleeve and hummed his settling song. He continued to search for things; matches, a stick of wood the right length and the little tin of paraffin he wore at his waist.

He heard the motorcycle thrum and steady, the boy's leg swinging happily over it with another job done. 'Eat well,' he called. 'See you tomorrow, perhaps.' His numberplate, Rolf noticed, watching him go, was exactly divisible by seventeen.

While he waited for his cup of water to boil, Rolf sat on the warm thick newspaper-and-plastic bench he'd made, to eat the last of the bread from his stopover at the bakery near Karlsruhe where he'd worked all night. Difficult swine, that baker. He'd been glad to leave before light, the money safe in his new boots, his strong teeth full of the stale knackwurst he'd taken from their wastebin.

He held his head where the pain was. The pain that came when he had to listen to people talking.

The boy pretending to come from the city offices must be mad. Why would Stuttgart give their money away? Everyone would stop working if they did. Too much talking in the world. How long since he had stopped talking? He swivelled round so that his bottom lifted from the dateline on the newspapers. October already. So, six months. Or eighteen months. Spring one year, anyway. A good spring it was, too hot for boots.

Only when the water had boiled and he'd counted every frothing bubble, when he'd poured a little away to make room for the powdered coffee, powdered milk and sugar he'd picked up from the last station buffet, when he'd stirred it thirty-four times to the left and watched the spirals equalize and merge, did he take out both the five-mark notes. Lovely. Lovely. He smoothed and smoothed the wonderful numbers on their corners until he had thoroughly examined them both. So many threes and so few sevens on them. The last two digits of one went fourteen times exactly into the last three of the other, the square root of the whole was . . . done, finished. Nothing more. Zero. He held them gratefully in his fingers for a moment then let the sharp wind blow them away towards him first, then under, through, over the railway bridge. Finders keepers.

Leaving his stove on guard and taking just his canvas satchel, Rolf collected all the timetables from the information desk at the station and was delighted to see a creased map of Stuttgart centre stuffed in a bin.

He replenished the coffees and milks and sugars before they called the station-master to puff up red and swear at him, pointing to the way out. Not yet. On a bench just inside the men's washroom, three tramps sat sharing two unlabelled bottles, one of them helpless with laughter, the other two just helpless. As his water trickled from him, Rolf looked at them with pity. However did you end up like that, he thought, tucking the four torn edges of his shirt back so he could zip up properly.

'Wanna drink, Kumpel?'

The hot water felt so nice, Rolf washed his hands twice and then once again. He didn't look at the men or in the mirror. He had stopped looking at himself the same day he stopped talking.

'Staying here the night, Kumpel?'

Rolf washed just once more, then wrapping his muffler twice round his neck, he put his canvas bag right over his shoulder.

'Get your ten marks today? Wanna join with us?

We're saving up for a Mercedes and then we'll travel the whole whole whole wide world.'

Their laughter and a last shout from someone coming towards him followed him down the outside steps back to his patch and along the road back to the tip. Rejecting mattress after mattress as being too smelly, too ripped, too thin, he finally found just the thing and rolled it quickly, moving swiftly out and down the road again, afraid as always after a find like this of being knocked down for it. Not today. Safe.

It was still three hours before the Stuttgart scholastic bookfair would be over at the Liederhall. Twenty-one thousand, six hundred half seconds. Five half-hours before he had to leave, according to the map he took from his satchel, lying full length on the mattress, his body completely covering the pink teddy-bears and orange flower-baskets of the ticking.

According to the map, if he walked towards the sky-tall television tower at an angle of seventy-three degrees, he'd pass the Zoological Gardens. It had been a long time since he'd seen any animals except cows by day and rats over his feet at night. Tomorrow he'd clean out cages for the keepers and maybe the next day, then, he could buy enough food to take him on to Munich. Choosing the timetable for Munich now that he had thought of it, he started to add every number on the first pages, then the total slipped sideways and fell waiting for him as he slept the sleep the bakery owed him.

Sitting on a low wall opposite the Stuttgarter Lieder-hall, Rolf smiled, watching the lights of the long, low building go out one by two, changing the percentage of lights on to those off too slowly for his enjoyment so that he had to play silent number games as well to keep from being bored. Longer than usual to shut down this book-fair. A series of six lights went off together towards the front of the hall; the secretaries must be finishing. More. More. All dark. Rolf began to count seconds. One sauerkraut. Two sauerkraut. Three sauerkraut. Three thousand, six hundred seconds to count before his hour of darkness rule.

Three thousand, five hundred and ninety-nine sauerkraut. The car-park was empty now. The night-watchman sat like he was sunning himself at Baden-Baden. 'Scraps in the bin,' he said, jerking his head at Rolf. 'Round the back. The big tall ones, the food's in. The flat one's only books, like. You've chose a good night. Too much food they bought, I think. What a waste. 'elp yourself, Kumpel. Don't kill yourself talkin', will yer.'

In the effort not to seem in a hurry, Rolf counted a slow rhythm for his legs and had taken eight hundred and fifty-six small steps, down the slope, up the wide stairs, round to the back and – look at that. His small torch blinked at the sight. The pulping bins were full to overflowing. Why, he'd never found out, but that's what they always did after bookfairs. Wasted them. Crushed all those lovely books. Rolf rescued what numbers he could, always.

Playing with Numbers straight into the canvas bag. *Modern Mathematics*, got it. *University Mathematics*, in the bag. *Elements of*, *Rudiments of*, not that orange-coloured *Mathematics and Logic* again. *Mathematics tomorrow*, nice, *Key to Mathematics*, yes, *Mathematics Re-examined*, no.

Not just books, but names on books of people just like Rolf. People who lived for numbers just like him. People like he had never met. Where were they? People it would be worth talking to.

One more dig in the last bin. Got that and that and two copies of that. Or something very like them. No more. One last poke about. *Puzzles for your calculator*,

Rolf pushed it away uninterested but it fell over the side and a slim, heavy, small slippery calculator fell out of a place inside, with a card 'For The Teacher of Advanced Mathematics This Book is Essential. Free calculator with every three dozen copies.'

Too dark to see what it was like. 'Sonnenzellen-Batterie,' it blazed. Solar. The sun. Of course. It would only work by day. He fingered it, shone his torch on the numbers. Well, a toy for the morning and throw it away after. He'd read of them in every one of his books. Well, he'd see in the morning. In the bag.

Footsteps. Rolf buckled the bag and strode fast to the big tall trash bin in time to be leaning appreciatively into it when the night-watchman's legs reached him. Rolf's hands brought out surprisingly fat parcels of food; genuinely astonished at such generous pickings he grunted towards the fellow and offered one to him.

'No, ta, I lives well. I gets it before it comes out 'ere. 'elp yourself. Good i'nt it? I tol' you.'

It was nearly noon when the motor-cycle pulled up under the bridge again and this time the boy stayed astride it, taking out a list. Not the same boy at all, Rolf finally looked up to notice, but surely his brother, the pimples starting and stopping in the same places amongst his fluffy stubble.

'Gut,' said the boy pointing approvingly to the food still beside Rolf from the night before. 'So, the money was well spent. No drink. Gut.' He made a note on his paper and took out two more green five-mark notes. 'Second day,' he said. 'And would you like, now, to look for a place to stay? Warm and dry? No? Tomorrow, maybe. Take them. Take them.' He leaned forward and put the waved-away notes into Rolf's coat-pocket, revved up and was gone.

So, if you wanted eight per cent of a number added to
– then you pressed six, four, nine, one, eight, seven,
four, say, times eight per cent then plus and there it was
to one decimal place, seven, zero, one, one, two, two,
three point nine and that was interesting, too, that zero,
one, two, three sequence in the middle.

Since there had been enough light to work the machine, Rolf had sat there, books ignored, hunger and
thirst forgotten, his legs stiffening under him, working,
working, sometimes faster than the machine, sometimes slower, only scared that it would wear out and
stop before he had mastered it. People passed; what if
you pressed 'times' twice? Or three times? What if?
Trains came in, drew out, tramps, tramps, tramps
struggled, straggled into town, the ten-mark wonder
calling them by grapevine from Bonn, from Bremen,
from Hamburg, even.

The older man who drew up with the ten marks in an
old repainted car the next day asked Rolf if he were well
and made many notes on his paper through the silence
and remarked that it was good to see that he had bought
plenty of food (the bin-leavings being mostly still beside
Rolf though staling a little) then he held out the money,
tucked it into Rolf's pocket and push-started his car on
to the next stop.

The young woman who came on Friday tried to wake
the tramps who had joined Rolf under the arch, ignored
the filth they called her as she handed them the money
and came to Rolf.

She made a face at the smell and told him that the
food was 'off' and to make sure to get some more with
today's money and did he want shelter for the week-end.
She shrugged with cold, wrote 'deaf?' on her pad, put the
money in his jacket and walked away not looking back.

After his money had been brought to him on

Monday, scarcely noticing his three new sleeping-partners, he walked stiffly under the Mercedes cross on the station, rustling with unspent money and with his calculator safe round his neck in a bag.

He walked unchallenged through the busy main platform to a larger washroom, stepping over half a dozen men, senseless on the floor, to get to a cubicle.

Clever Stuttgart had emptied the rest of Germany of their tramps.

He locked the door, sat down and waited patiently. Holding a hand to his chest he felt the heavy little smooth calculator warm-cold against his breastbone and smiled. It was like having a friend with more numbers in his head than he had. He had begun to talk to it, praising it when it did well, jealous if it did very well. He felt busy, important, happy with the calculator to work with. He felt – he felt very hungry.

Hungry. How long since he'd eaten? A few days? A few weeks? Perhaps he would, after all, use some of the Stuttgart marks for food because there would be no time to work if he was to get through that book of calculator workings. Now he had worried out what the memory buttons did, he could count his steps every day and add it in and at the end of the year, he would know how far a man can travel away from home on foot and then you could calculate – well, anything, couldn't you? The hundreds of calculator books he'd discarded in the past pressed on the pain in his head again and he held it so it didn't explode.

A door slammed back, three, four whistles whistled, men stomped, instructions were shouted, drunken swearing was answered by sober swearing. Rolf held his breath.

Suddenly, a shout of pain and rage, running, doors flung back again, a gun went off, the Stuttgart police were cleaning up the mess the do-gooders had made. Rolf waited where he was, though they banged and yelled for the doors to be opened. Someone was groaning. Someone was lifted away. Silence.

When he unlocked the door and peered out cautiously, the eyes of the tramp in the next cubicle were only inches away from his. They both laughed as if they were the only two left in the world and laughed again for nothing in the quietness of the empty washroom.

There was fresh blood on the floor. They could both see it. They stepped over it.

'Spent your ten marks today?' the other fellow said, hands in the pocket of a coat far dirtier and more torn than Rolf's but with very superior boots.

Rolf let the hot water play and play over his hands in pleasure and delight. Water. He would do that one day. Swim. He would swim in water that fell from your shoulders as you stood to dive again.

'I said have you spent it. Spent them. Have you?' The fellow stood nearer, squarely, too close.

Rolf shook his head, the water forming seventeen per cent more bubbles on the left hand than the right and . . .

'Give it me,' the man said, accompanying the request with a punched hand to Rolf's lungs, 'or I'll . . .' Every hit seemed to reach through to his back, he was bursting, his hands up to protect his throat, he was open, he was down, he was . . .

Other men, stepping over him and his spilled blood to get to the urinals understandably took him for another drunken sot the town was suffering, cursing him, threatening him as he came slowly to consciousness.

No need to check if his food money had gone. The fellow had simply swopped coats with him, added

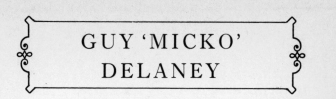

GUY 'MICKO' DELANEY

Desmond Hogan

I

'Your Dad was no good. Your Dad was no good, boy.'
Guy grew up from an early age hearing these words. Yet
his father's name was implanted in the middle of his
names. 'Micko'. Guy 'Micko' Delaney. He always bowed his head to the information. He got used to this
gesture. A boy of seventeen in 1960 he wore a red shirt
with black roosters suffused in it, a shirt he'd got in
Dublin. He had black hair and a little alarming bit of
acne on his left cheek which when it was gone later left a
dent. There were green trees, lots of them, near the
little cottage where he lived with his mother on the hill,
green trees tucked around the Protestant church and the
head of the Protestant church seeming to look into their
home, the four spired head of the squat Protestant
church. 'Aspens, we have aspens growing near us,' his
mother would say. A squat person herself, her cheeks
the colour of beet, a floral navy pinafore on her, daisies
on Sundays, bindweed flowers on weekdays. She was a
char in people's homes. Guy was a good for nothing
many attested but it wasn't quite true; he'd worked in a
funeral parlour, with a blacksmith, on the roads – as a
labourer. His father had had each of these jobs too. The
blacksmith owned a coach, which had once belonged to
the last lord of the local manor and which was in his
possession now, displaying it in the backyard where
gates opened onto the street, on sunny days which also
gave him and his helpers the opportunity to display
their chests to the populace, the most interested people,
in either their chests or the coach, being children and

[161]

not the cleanest of children either, children who were likely to have lice in their hair. 'Lice' was a preoccupation then. Guy had been born during the war. The night of a famous sea-battle. His father had already been away at war.

Even though he had a reputation for bravado he was humble of speech, of gesture, back slightly arched. Girls loved him, and so did his mother. They'd spend many nights together. Just sitting on a sofa. Talking. The fire on and roaring, a reflection of it, into a picture of a ship on the sea, which looked like a ship on churning Guinness because the picture was all brown. The innuendo here was the sea. The sea-battle Guy was born during. The sea-battles in films in the cinema which Guy watched through a peep-hole in the Men's Club above the cinema, a hole you could peek through and also watch lovers' lips meeting in black and white. Guy always seemed to leave a billiard game and peek down just as lovers' lips met.

The Men's Club was a point of contention. A place away from the life he shared with his mother. Girls were a point of grief and outrage. The conversations at the side of the ballroom; girls taken to the middle of the green in summer. Guy talked about art with girls at the side of the ballroom or in the middle of the fair green. He also talked about paths of escape. Smoke in the Men's Club was decisive avenues into the air.

Mrs Delaney smiled a lot. She smiled on her way to a house where she worked. She dispensed merriment at funerals. She couldn't help wearing a smile almost to the moment when she shook hands with somebody in sympathy. She also smiled when she started attending sessions with a lady doctor in the local mental hospital, smiled on her way to these sessions. She was suffering from 'Nerves' and she spoke about this disease as if she'd been conferred with an honour. 'Nerves'. The source of 'nerves' maybe was Guy's increasing times away; sessions, conversation sessions with girls in the middle of the fair green.

'Your father was no good.' The words were muffled into dialogue heard from the cinema. It was the Men's Club. The urinal. A man brushed against Guy. 'Don't go his way.' Which way? What route? There was still tenderness between Guy and his mother; they'd go to a pub sometimes together and sit in an alcove, talking. Their heads often inclined closely together. It some-times seemed Mrs Delaney was going to drink out of Guy's pint. A woman would rustle in to see if they were all right. 'More sherry?' A peek at the physical close-ness, at Mrs Delaney's lap, at the narrow black trousers on Guy. 'O there's a man here, all the way from Athlone tonight, and he says there'll be Jehovah Witnesses coming here. A gang of them. Not nice. Disgraceful. Who are they? Are they the Salt Lake City crowd? Salt Lake City, I had an aunt who visited there on her way to California.' A hand goes down for an empty sherry glass not divined before. 'O Mrs Delaney you look like a million dollars.' And Mrs Delaney would beam like the leprechaun on a jug over her mantelpiece.

On the mantelpiece there were ginger cocker spa-niels; there was a family of pigmies; there was a con-torted-looking iron candlestick holder, all kinds of patterns embroiled in it; there was a picture of the Virgin Mary, a rainbow arcing over her. There was a message from Hollywood, a postcard with a bubble of dialogue coming out from a film-star's mouth. Some-thing about 'across the miles'. A surrogate message from a relative in California. Then there was the leprechaun jug of course and a huge bunch of green plastic leaves in a vase, white with four lines of blue, protruding dots on

its sides. Also there were the Lakes of Killarney in a
snow-storm ball. Killarney had been where Mrs Delaney and Micko had gone on their honeymoon.

Jehovah Witnesses came to town. Men in dark suits.
They scoured the houses for souls. Then they went to
the ballroom that night and met Guy to whom they
talked about greyhound meetings. They'd been to a
great greyhound meeting in Dublin. They were not
from Salt Lake City but from Liverpool. Mrs Geraghty, the mad woman, who still lamented a husband
killed in a tractor accident years before, gave them a
calendar although it was March. There were green trees
around the Protestant church all year round, pines, firs,
but in March further green came, aspens, oaks. Mrs
Geraghty's calendar had no picture attached to it and
was in plain, scarlet letters. That calendar said March
1961 now. Guy, having been born in February, was
eighteen.

'Well you can't help being your father's son. A queer
hawk.' A man frothed over a pint, the froth like the
white tumescence created by opening leaves, on the
glass. The man's eyes dived to the ground. He'd give
nothing away.

Mrs Delaney died that May in the mental hospital
while she was receiving electric shock treatment. She'd
been talking about the treatment for weeks, building up
to it, readying everybody for it. It was going to be a
great event. But on a day when oak leaves rubbed
against the grey mental hospital building she died. But
the scandal was, the scandal that lives to this day, Guy
played billiards in the Men's Club that night.

Guy stayed on in the cottage for a few years after his
mother's death. He led a solitary life. He sometimes
brought girls there. People didn't like him now although he was given the part of Jimmy Brown in a spot

[164]

in the Saint-Patrick's-night concert. 'In the Valley the Bells are Ringing.' Guy sang the main part with a chorus of girls from the hosiery factory in what looked like holy communion frocks behind him. Guy worked for a while in the hosiery factory.

He sometimes stood in Gertrude's Fish and Chip Shop, under the picture of John XXIII, chatting to Gertrude. Gertrude had been to South Africa and had come back to open the fish and chip shop.

It was no surprise when he went; he sold the cottage and took off. A woman who inhabited a pair of man's pyjamas moved in, staring out at people, a pale owlish face among russet hair, pink and white striped pyjamas on her. She'd sometimes bellow through a window partially open in summer, 'You should be home by now,' to little boys scampering across the hill at evening or little boys enjoying the space under the Protestant trees, a luxuriance above and lots of earnest flies.

Guy first went to London; he wrote to friends about films, two Russian films. *Ivan the Terrible* and *The Boyars' Plot* where in one or the other of those films the screen bursts from black and white to colour. He'd become arty. Letters were peppered by artiness and descriptions of girlfriends whose bee-hive hair-dos were saddled by the tiniest of chiffon scarves. Afterwards came South Africa. References. *Bloutrein. Slegs Vir Blankes*. Descriptions of white Dutch colonial houses in Cape Town. Of a vantage-point from where you could see the Atlantic ocean meet the Indian ocean. The bar lady who'd been solicitous to his mother and himself got a packet of porridge, *Ekonomie Pak*, and she kept going around for weeks in the pub, showing it to customers, to strangers even, trying to find out the meaning of this conundrum. And what Guy spoke most about to the odd friend, a little boy he'd known who used to scamper over the hill and who'd sit with him on a red bench on the hill, was those journeys on steam-trains through the countryside. South Africa still had steam-trains, the steam going up and alarming, triggering the movement of giraffes. 'Gold,' he spoke about too. 'I've found gold. I've found jazz.' Ironically in a land of oppression Guy had discovered a jazz club where blacks and whites convened and where messages were beaten out in jazz music, in the signals of cigarette smoke. In this club he met a man from home who'd known his father and who told him he had a step-brother in London, a son his father had had by a Ukranian girl from Liverpool.

The man had treated the encounter as casually as he might have a Sunday night encounter in a pub at home. He was a sailor. He was used to meeting people known to him or vaguely remembered by him, in Cape Town, Rio de Janeiro, Santiago. There was a greyness about his face despite the fact he'd been on the sea for years, his hair also grey. He'd lived in London in the late forties, returning home for a while in the early fifties. He remembered Guy as a boy. 'You haven't changed son.' There was a spillage of colour down Guy's face then, from the sun, blues, reds, his hair all curly in front, not the peaked front of the early sixties. He had in a sense returned to his boy's face. Now he left South Africa, researching his brother. The man had told him that his brother was an auctioneer in London and worked mainly in the art world. He gave him the name of an art firm. Guy found him within weeks. It was 1970.

At first Guy stayed in the Tavistock Hotel in Tavistock Square. Then he found a council flat in Hornsey. That was meant to be a temporary home but it became permanent and it's still his address. When he made to go back to South Africa a few years later he wasn't allowed back – some political misdemeanour during his years there – he was tricked by his quest into being trapped in London for ever. And his brother, at first refusing to see him, then seeing him, ultimately shut the door on him and had nothing to do with him. So Guy had Hornsey and memories of South Africa and a quest now for his father and himself.

Jonathan. That was Guy's brother's name. And as far as Guy was concerned he sounded like a Jonathan. Very English. Upper-class accent. Remote from people with accents like Guy's. And then there was his appearance. Blond hair falling in a generous sweep on a face that was salmon-coloured, and eyes and lips that were, to Guy, 'peckish', particular. There was also a saccharine pink about those tiny lips. And the first time, the first encounter, those lips opened to disdain Guy. Jonathan didn't want to know. There was a legend of his father who'd died in 1947; there was a legend of a town which had a cattle-trough decorated with cypress trees at a juncture of its streets. But otherwise Jonathan's mother had wanted to forget. And Jonathan had gone along with the gesture.

Guy hung on in London – old acquaintances, old friends – he moved into the council flat. He sent the address to his brother. Then one Christmas his brother invited him to his flat in Maida Vale. The invitation came on a printed card. Guy had to r.s.v.p.

He'd waited for rejection to be revoked. He was excited. He dressed up. He dressed up to look as well as he had at his mother's funeral. He worked in a carpet shop. Just off the day before, Christmas Eve, he decorated himself now, grease in his hair so he looked like a 1960s' teddyboy, navy suit with an electric sheen in it, dun and yellow check tie, white shirt, tie-pin with an

Armada ship in it his mother had given him. He set off
for Maida Vale on foot because there was no public
transport at Christmas, crossing the bridge on Hornsey
Lane from which you could see all of London, Archway
Road beneath him. The first thing he noticed in the
room was the Christmas cards. Cards lavish and often
with gold letters in them. Men in dinner jackets stood
about, pudgy, almost emblematic stomachs on them.
Young men sauntered up to them and squeaked their
credentials at them. There were women in low-cut
black dresses, and the acknowledgement of Ireland was
stacks of John McCormack records that Guy sat beside,
a custodian. People came and went but few talked to
Guy. They looked at him as if he had burst in from a
fancy dress party, as if he was a runaway from a country
and western jamboree. At his mother's funeral Guy had
worn a blue suit but it had the same electric sheen in it.
What was extraordinary, what was immemorial in his
home-town was an embarrassment here. Guy crouched
in a corner, a bunch of embarrassment. After dinner,
after champagne and beaujolais nouveau, he threw up
in the bathroom. He'd been drinking hot chocolate all
day to avoid getting drunk. Now chocolate covered
white-washed walls, photographs of stone-walls
(another acknowledgement of Ireland, albeit a lavato-
rial one).

Guy left, crossing broken glass on Edgware Road,
walking all the way home. From then on it was priests,
nuns, Irish clubs, and a carpet shop. He didn't go
home. There was no home to go to.

Jonathan insisted on a few encounters after that and
treated Guy scientifically almost during these encounters, as if he was checking out some details for the
benefit of some of his own research. He came to the flats
in a taxi one day, the taxi veering into the courtyard and

[168]

Jonathan getting out in a black coat. Guy saw him from the seventh floor. They had red wine – this was about the second time Guy had met him since the Christmas party, it was summer – and Jonathan said to Guy, 'You know he's buried in Willesden. Our mutual father. I went to the graveyard once. You better hurry if you want to catch it. It's fading away.' Then, looking closely at Guy, he said, 'Someone said after the party, you had a good face. She'd like to have painted you.' Guy remembered a huge painting in Jonathan's, all colours in it, like sequins. 'Would you be interested? A portrait?'

'No.'

'You don't want to be Dorian Gray then?'

A strange remark because Guy had never aged.

'No.'

Jonathan said, 'Sorry. These things don't work.' And he left. Before he went to the door he turned. 'My mother died from drugs you know. I was adopted. It complicates things. Puts us at a remove. And by the way you do have a good face.'

Jonathan came back a few times to see Guy's face and Guy realized he was looking at his father's face, as if at a death-mask.

'I've lost my gold. I've lost my jazz.' Guy wrote to a friend in Ireland, the boy he'd known, who was now in Dublin. 'In South Africa, despite war, despite oppression, people help one another, people come close. Here closeness is difficult, closeness is tantamount to danger. In South Africa people, poor people, knocked their tin kettles together and made jazz.'

And thinking of jazz, thinking of films that burst from black and white to colour, the last time he saw his brother, after his brother had gone, Guy had thought 'I'm an artist too.'

And as an artist, although a carpet salesman as well,

he reconstructed the story of his father, whose ignominy was in his middle name. He wrote it all down eventually and sent it back to Ireland as if that gesture, sending it to someone from his town who was now in Dublin, would cleanse him of some guilt. 'O he played billiards the night his mother died. He's his father's son.'

Guy was his father's son and strangely found that an agreeable and a creative state.

The priests and nuns were all from a local church and the confraternities associated with it; there was a hall, there were meetings. Someone had once warned Guy, in Dublin in fact, on his way out of Ireland, 'You always go back. You always go back to the roots you were born to.' And Guy was here in a church hall, balloons above him, and Irish voices around him. He looked bewildered now. Out of place. First Christmas after the party in his brother's. But shortly after Christmas he visited his father's grave. There was an Indian restaurant nearby and Guy had a curry first. It was a Monday. He had a day off work. Christmas decorations still clung to a goldfish tank; trailed over it, blue with silver edges. The graveyard looked like a field in Ireland in January, dead earth, an iron sky above it. In an anorak Guy found the grave and as he stared at it he thought of goldfish; goldfish flicking their tails, goldfish as a luxuriance, goldfish as little stellar beings in the gloom of an Indian restaurant, in the gloom of a cemetery. And in the cemetery he heard Mrs Buchanan's voice from the Christmas party, 'I've got you in my clutches now and I won't let you go.'

They went to Killarney on their honeymoon in 1939.
Mrs Delaney had saved up for it by working as a cham-
ber-maid in a hotel in Clifden Connemara. 'Why didn't
you go to Clifden,' someone asked. 'Because Killarney
is more romantic.' And Mrs Delaney and Micko danced
to 'I love you just the same Sweet Adeline' in a hotel in
Killarney on a moonlit night just about the time the war
broke out. Micko was in a navy suit with a sheen in it,
his hair very black, almost a tail at the end of it, 'like a
pirate's'. She was small, pudgy even then. 'My little
apple-pie', he called her and that was an ominous title,
too domestic. She glowed. There was an extraordinary
amount of shades of red in her face. No one could deny
his beauty, partly a beauty that came from the roads on
which he sometimes worked as a labourer, a dexterity of
limb, culminating in a pale face which had ragged dark
eyes in it. She protected him and she loved him. Even
when it turned out she had to work to support him.
When he played billiards in the Men's Club and didn't
come home until late. When he stood on the road, a
labourer, his shirt off, and had Betty Croffey, proprie-
tress of the San Diego Cafe and Fruit Stores stare at him
– she the sister of a church prelate in San Diego, thus
the name. Micko seemed to take a strange energy from
the roads on which he worked, often roads bearing
colonial names; India Avenue; he was most at home on
Crimea Avenue where gladioli jumped up in the
gardens in summer and doctors' daughters peeked over
the gladioli at him. There was also the old workhouse as
a favourite background, it conjured history behind his
naked chest. There was a little array of oak trees near the
workhouse, on the opposite side of the road, flanking

one another evenly in summer when they were in bloom. This was a favourite stalking ground for Micko. There was something nubile about his naked chest and Betty Croffey, not known to look very much at men, stared at it in fixation, a mirage of pink wool on the side of the road. But Mrs Delaney bore her rivals with ease. Micko had come out of the basest slums of town, cottages behind the Catholic church; there was an interesting poison about him for people like Betty Croffey. But for her it was love and devotion. Even if Micko sometimes stood in the middle of the road, shirt off, trying to procure admirers. Then when he discovered his wife was pregnant he was off. To the war. 'Bye. See you. I've got to fight to make a living for you and our child. Nothing doing here. This place is a dungeon for the working man.' Micko joined the British army and in 1944 gradually moved in on Hitler – he was going to put Hitler in the socket with a billiard club. Names, names thrown in the air like confetti, that's what Mrs Delaney had back; Dunkirk, Normandy, the Rhine Valley, Berlin. Guy was two then. He was walking when Micko rode down Budapester Strasse on a motorbike, a girl on the back, and children waved at him, oak trees in bloom despite the ruination of the street, a little boy waving a hankie and other children picking up broken-away, leafy bits of the oak trees and waving them, light in them, exploding him into a sudden purpose – yes, he'd come to liberate his posterity, his son from the dungeon of Ireland, to create a precedent for him, a way out, new countries. There'd be no going back now because he, Micko, had seen this, a manifestation of renewal in this war-capsized city. And with this hopeful realization he returned to England, took up with a Ukrainian girl from Liverpool who was pregnant from an American GI and lived in a room in Crouch End with her, an ikon of the Virgin and Child on the wall, the Hornsey Valley below the garden, pear trees in the garden.

Cocaine Bill and Morphine Sue
Were walking down the avenue
Afterwards she swore he was on strange drugs.

Micko sang a lot, the hit songs of the day, and when she had a blond-haired boy he became morose and started stalking London at night, playing billiards in a men's club.

One night on his way home from the club he saw dancers on the street, a GI dancing with two girls outside a jazz club, an old lady standing on the pavement, waiting for a partner, and he danced with the old lady, danced until ghosts from his town trooped across the sky, the man who was hanged by the local landlord because he'd stolen a cabbage, the Cockney music hall artiste who'd married a later landlord, the ghosts suddenly arrested in their movement and jiving in the sky until it was too bright for any further such fantasy.

Micko walked home. There was no one there. He'd forgotten. He took off his suit and pulled a chair to him, back to front, and sat there, an artist's model, sleeveless white cord vest on him with yawning niches in it, and savoured the morning there, the light from the pears outside, and suddenly the light, brushstroke upon brushstroke of it, exploding and putting him back in Berlin so the chair became the motorbike and the pear trees the oak trees and he was riding down Budapester Strasse with the girl, a volley of children at the side of the street, waving, and that little boy, thick, brown hair on him, a frail smile, boots that had no laces, his son. That boy was his son. Micko recognized him now. He'd run away from home so he could encounter his child. There was a mirthful recognition.

Guy was four when his father died. They closed the Men's Club that night. No one played billiards there. The ship on the sea in the cottage had a black ribbon over it and a red rose at the end of it. The leprechaun on the jug wept, the tears getting on his emerald dicky-bow.

Micko looked even closer and saw that this boy wasn't just his son but other children he'd run away for, he'd opened doors for; there were other children, retinues and retinues of them, like flanks of biblical trees, after his son. Micko had performed a heroic deed. He'd gone through some time-barrier in Berlin in August 1945 and caught sight of the children who were going to be born in the town he came from long after he was dead. He'd created a bit of hope for them like other people made vests at the local factory. Not so much because he'd run away but because, by default, he'd experienced this, Berlin, a great city, in its worst disarray, and yet children here and leaves and light hitting off the topmost leaves the way light hit off stained glass in a church. If you like, he thought, he'd planted an oak tree for his son and the children that would come after him, that would be in their intuitive knowledge, in their deepest memories, and, even at their worst moments, there'd be no going back on those memories. He'd got to the other side of destruction.

The light in the leaves of the broken away bits of oak tree exploded and Micko was back in London, traversing the gardens in the Hornsey Valley at the back of the house where he had a room, going downwards, his feet almost seeming not to touch the ground, his route taking him past a white, round temple of a garden-house, the walking becoming more like swimming and Micko lying down, but not before he saw his son, aged four, a trophy on his shoulders, not before he saw his son linked up in this chain of life.

Guy looked at the grave and shuddered in the January cold. It was a spot his mother had visited in attending Micko's funeral. It had been a quiet funeral. And afterwards all she could talk about was how, weeks later she mysteriously got Micko's dicky-bow sent to her in a shoe box. There had been a strange congregation at this grave though, Mrs Delaney, a Ukrainian girl from Liverpool, a potential brother. Secrets had been transacted here that still made a cabalistic energy in the air and Guy was loath to leave the energy, to tear himself away from it. It was a comfort. So much of his past was here, the voice of his mother.

So ultimately to comfort himself he wrote to Dublin that night. The screen burst from black and white to colour that January day, a story created for another person, the figure who'd stood in the cemetery suddenly remembering he'd worn red shirts once and colouring them in in his descriptions to make someone else, in turn, remember. There'd been an incandescence at a graveyard and that night an attempt at art, at putting the colours inside the ikon, and jazz was heard again and shared with another person, the way it had been in letters in the mid-sixties fresh on the trail of an agonized and uncertain moment of exit.

3

London by bicycle is a strange place. You skirt, you dart about, you are a spectre here, a bit of a white shirt there, the back of a red bike somewhere else, connecting things, drawing them up for yourself, involving yourself in a story again, trying to placate the bits and pieces again, trying to calm down elements of them that flare up unreasonably. The man cycled around London on a January day, past Friern Barnet where he was recently in the mental hospital, past Hornsey where he stayed with Guy when he first came to London, on to Maida Vale where he befriended Jonathan for a while, to Willesden where he visited Micko's grave, then stopping by a bandstand in a park in Hampstead.

Everything in this city has the possibility of downfall; a corner bar, an avenue of brand-new council flats, a bandstand. Everything has been touched, been fondled by that possibility. But something has held you back. Something has come between you and it.

What held you back? God knows.

The first time he met Guy was by Shallow Horseman's. Guy used to go there to swim. His figure crunched up in black and white striped swimming togs on the bank. Guy's mother worked for the boy's mother for a while as a char and, with this pretext of intimacy, Guy once lifted the boy on his shoulders when he'd come there in a drove of children, after talking to him about ladybirds – one at the boy's heels – and carried him into the water, buttercups on the side of the river, the boy screaming, screeching, Guy saying there were alligators down there, the boy laughing. And then Guy brought him back safely to the bank and deposited him there, but not before saying 'Please, don't let me forget,' not verbally, but in his eyes.

Lots of stuff you forget. Guy's forgotten now. He's married with children, still working in the carpet shop, but also working for the homeless at night and at weekends, a job he procured through priests and nuns.

Lots of things you forget but not everything, the man

will never forget the rosebuds in Mrs Delaney's wallpaper when he went to her house on her invitation and found her sitting on a sofa with Guy, yellow curtains behind them, gold storks in the curtains. He took a photograph in his mind and the photograph still endures, like one of the photographs on Mrs Delaney's mantelpiece, caressed as they were by an artificial weed, a ribbon. That was the man's one time there. But it was enough. There was a quiet war going on then between Guy and herself. The woman left the employment of the boy's mother and his relationship with Guy ceased for a few years, until he used to scamper over the hill and find him on a red bench. They'd sit, talking there, looking at the perspective of the fair green. Then Guy's mother died and there was even more scandal than there had been before about Guy. But the relationship went on. And they planned things together and talked about art and bound one another to some quiet, unstated fidelity. Guy left. Last time the boy saw him was in the Town Hall at a production of Michael Macliammoir's *Ill met by Moonlight*, a woman wandering about the stage in a blue négligé entranced. Guy too was entranced, by his decision to leave. There was an abundance in that decision. He went far away and then somehow became trapped in London, got caught there in what was meant to be a temporary sojourn. Then the boy didn't hear from him for years until pages came, pages and pages talking about his father. And the boy wrote back on a postcard. The postcard showing O'Connell Street in the fifties. The boy and his mother met Guy and his mother on that street about the late fifties when Guy and his mother had come out of *Darby O'Gill and the Little People* at the Metropole Cinema. Again, almost always, there was some item of art in the meetings, in the exchanges, a backdrop on the Town

Hall stage; leprechauns leaping around the Metropole screen; descriptions from London of films that burst from black and white to colour; descriptions of jazz from South Africa; then an ultimate bit of art from Guy, pages about his father. An invitation coming with the pages for the boy to move to London. The boy, the young man as he was then, did move to London. He didn't stay long with Guy. But it was the beginning of the odyssey, of the trek through London which brought him to this bandstand where he'd halted with his bicycle now.

Jonathan visited the town. He stayed in the main hotel. There was one shop window on the main street, a shop which had closed in the forties, with placards from the forties still in it, a woman with ice-blond hair sipping champagne, a velvet-blue night in Paris. This was not his town. He was not from here. He was from somewhere in Arizona or Minnesota.

The young man met him in a pub in Warwick Place in Maida Vale while he lived in that area. Jonathan recognised the accent. He sat on a bench as though he was a peer of the pub. It was very benign September weather outside. 'You're Irish.' Jonathan had just been to the young man's town that summer. And connections were made. There were instant invitations. Jonathan was a man who'd never aged, blond hair, a pool of it on either side of his forehead, broad, sportsman's shoulders, a pale jersey very often, with pink outlines of very jolly and very brotherly little waves at the bottom of it; lots of items around him, jugs, silver-ware, paintings, a crescendo on the broad mantelpiece, carpets of crimson. Jonathan still wanted to find a way back to the town he'd visited that summer, despite the fact that the air there did not possess a sense of paternity for him, and he talked and talked about it, things he'd noticed, the

monument to the Protestant archbishop's two grey-
hounds, the workhouse which had partly been con-
verted into a disco now, the black shade of a bridge on a
river-side mill and on the river on a day which was
otherwise consumed by heat, the smell of icy ancient-
ness coming from that shade; all these things were like
paintings he wanted to purchase but couldn't get hold of
somehow. The young man might have been a good
liaison for a possible purchase. Spurred on by meeting
Jonathan, the young man went back to see Guy whom
he hadn't met for a few years. But, with children of his
own now, Guy had changed. A quiet war between him
and his mother once, a quiet relationship between him
and the boy once, there was a quiet forgetting now, a
quiet abnegation of backdrops in the Town Hall, of
Russian films, of jazz in a South African jazz club which
mixed up images of giraffes with steam trains, of a land
of oppression which still yielded nuances of harmony,
the border-line, dream-time memories of it. After an
unsatisfactory encounter with Guy there was just Jonathan then. But the young man spilt a bottle of beaujolais
nouveau on the crimson carpet one night, Christmas
night in fact, and knew he'd never be invited back. But
before he left the very formal, festive party, he noticed
in a corner of an alcove, littler than he'd imagined, an
ikon of Virgin and Child.

The mental hospital; yes, you suffered from 'nerves'
just like Mrs Delaney. But something kept you going.
What? Here you are.

The man paused on his bicycle beside the bandstand,
long enough so the moment would rebound in his mind,
bandstand, bicycle, his own figure, the sudden intensity
of the contemplativeness on his face.

A white bandstand, the smell of wet wood, the re-
proach, the impeachment of an almost lost sense of

some paternity, some father; the smell of a wet bandstand in January akin to the smell of semen; wood now
throttled by weather, by injurious dank.

Who are you? Why? All these over-indulged questions. Time to abandon them now. Time to go on. But
before leaving the path by the bandstand the man
looked straight in front of him as if someone was watching him, as if he was casting a querulous eye on a
stranger. But no one was there.

When Jonathan walked up the hill towards the cottage a woman was standing outside, an old woman,
wearing a nightdress, with a black dicky-bow around
her neck, hollering.

The man skid down a road between Hampstead and
Camden Town on his bike.

What was she hollering about? Micko Delaney. She'd
loved him once when he'd take his shirt off in the middle
of the road.

And by a little street into Camden Town. Apocalyp-
tic pictures of ANC fighters on the walls, a flotilla of
guns against a daisy-white sun and a daisy-white light.

'In the countryside, the Afrikaaner countryside, I
saw a tree, gnarled like a human being in pain. But it
still possessed music. The tree seemed to join its hands
in prayer. But it was still a beautiful sight; there's a
music here, a jazz, despite oppression. Long may it live
I say, the jazz. May it last for ever. I've found something
here, despite the terribleness of the country which I
hope will never leave me. There's a kind of golden light
in the air, a kind of rambling song that comes out of
oppression and out of beauty and out of sensuality, out
of shedding clothes, out of nudity. I was nude on a
beach one day and greeted the waves.' Letters written in
the late sixties, fast on the heels of letters written about
scarlet posters for Russian films in London.

[180]

At night this city is lonely. People are crowded by loneliness. Throngs of the homeless walk by the Thames. By the Thames there is an esplanade of homelessness. The man stopped somewhere near there that night, on his bicycle.

'In South Africa despite war, despite oppression people help one another,' Guy wrote once, 'People come close. People knock their tin kettles together.' He repeated that phrase more than once. Here there is a war too, a war with the spirit of the times.

Of late the man had spent some of his nights with the young homeless, a not very serious stay but serious enough to come close again, to start flowing again, to call on the Afrikaaner nether-worlds again, the Berlin oak trees which go hand in hand with war ruins.

You've got to try; try to start moving again, try to start flowing. And bring other things, other people with you. Ease that blockage, that jamming of memory that can cause so much pain; go back, even if it's to a moment before birth, a moment, an intuition which protected you. A bicycle was safely taken in for the night.

He took the bicycle down a long corridor which could have been a corridor in a mental hospital; Mrs Delaney's mental hospital, his own. But at the end there was a black and white photograph of a tree in bloom.

Outside you were aware of people shuffling against one another, those who had nowhere to go, nowhere to lay their heads tonight, the phantoms of South Africa; a boy in an orange sweater walking among those South African phantoms, yourself when young and receiving letters from Guy, yourself who was going to remedy the world. But no world laid itself open to you to be remedied; instead you gradually broke down, a mosaic splintering from its totality. You followed others. There was a lineage in falling apart.

A moment of hesitation, curling up, not wanting to go on, not wanting to be foolish – then a threshold is crossed and bonds are made; with a jazz club in Cape Town, a cabalistic conversation about ancestry; with lights in the Liffey in Dublin, day trips to Dublin which seemed to verge on the import of letters from South Africa; a porthole of a window in a mental hospital, sometimes the cavity in your life, sometimes a medieval window through which you saw strangenesses churn and circumstances change. The quest, having been grounded for a while, is starting all over again, the last flicker of a sunset washing in on the Pacific – or was it the Indian Ocean? – as seen from a Cape Town jazz club in a tumble of streets and rocks in some handed down version.

In a large room young people moved, like priests of a strange religion, around fires, they looked as if they were devoted to the fires, greens, purples dumped into hair, a graffiti of tattoos on an alarmingly nubile arm, untampered with, blond hair fluffed out, incandesced. And somewhere in the middle of the night the combustion of stories of escape from Carlisle, Leeds, Birmingham, Easingwold, Uig, the combustion of sympathy, created him, Micko, black suit on him, hat way back on his head, gold tie on him, but the man was no longer afraid of him, of the Micko part of himself, and could smile with ease at him, a young man in the last of the night singing a folk song he's learnt in Uig on the Isle of Skye, others sleeping, heads tipping towards the warmth of fires, the words smashing out, the adrenalin of fire in them, drawing all other stories hitherto heard in life into a single, beloved story, into a single, beloved mosaic, slightly awry and seared where the pieces joined up but adamant in this, turning lonely sleep from black and white to gold.

Outside in the street a few homeless people still shuffled, a woman with a huge scarf on her head, Byzantine patterns in it, stood over a fire, a few last ensembles lingered in conversation, and a young man in mock-forties clothes, hat way back on his head, listened to jazz coming from the radio of an all-night cafe before walking home, the nightmare gone now, nothing coming between you and the recognition of something that wasn't just an unhinged part of you but loving and self-sacrificial father to you, nothing coming between you and the lucid morning when the rumps of fleeing giraffes, zebras, last night's dreams, still flashed, a young man pulling a chair to him, back to front, the tops of his labourer's arms swathed in light, contemplating not pear trees or death but a scrawny bunch of purple crocuses, an ex-girl-addict's attempt to link up with the green of the spring.

Mrs Delaney put the dicky-bow in a brown envelope and hid it in a drawer, producing it to show to select visitors or as a talisman in her war for her son's affections. Micko's name was implanted in the middle of his son's names, as a memorial, to brand his son. But he was remembered anyway and is still remembered by the people who grew up in the town the decade after he died, in much the same way as they remember a folk song or the oak trees that used to bloom near the workhouse, oak trees that were cut down at a later point in their childhoods.

These days as Guy is almost forgotten, except for the chagrin of some distant scandal, it is Micko who is remembered. Moments real or imaginary of his life. Like the moment when they found his body late on that

August day, in his vest, and they didn't know how he died, and an English nurse wondered how this man, an Irishman, had an ikon on his wall, so exotic an emblem, radiating purples and reds and golds now as it caught the valley-edge sunset, being enhanced much as it would at evening on a cupboard in its home country. And it's moments like this, like the words of a folk song, like the memory of oak trees in bloom, like the mantra of items on a mantelpiece, that carry you forward, regardless.

A CHRISTMAS CORDIAL

Laura Kalpakian

Among the family there prevailed the sentiment that Louisa Wyatt ought somehow to have 'done something' with her life, though quite what remained unspecified since she had not done the obvious thing and got married. At least those closest to her used to express such thoughts, but gradually everyone who had known Louisa as a lively girl, an ebullient Oxford student, as a capable intelligent young woman had died off or emigrated and those who remained viewed her without that benign veil of youth or promise, in short, as a potty old woman of rigid habits and vague ways, she of the battered Burberry, the mothy scarf and galoshes, the hat pulled down tight over wiry, white hair, she who enjoyed alarmingly good health for her three-quarters of a century, who persisted in working part time when she might have retired ten years before, who lived all alone in an enormous house in Holland Park bequeathed to her by her parents where she fussed with ancient cookbooks and tended (in her own potty fashion) a large herb garden that had got away from her; the thyme ran wild, the sage and celandine quarreled, the basil died every summer for want of sunlight and the mint reigned supreme.

Certainly her cousin Enid (second or third cousin, Louisa had lost track) thought it unfair that Louisa should have an enormous, unattached four-storey house with rooms galore when Enid, her dyspeptic husband and her numerous brood were jammed, crammed, boxed and burrowed into considerably lesser quarters in Shepherd's Bush. Mr Basil Shillingcote, the solicitor who represented Louisa's affairs (for a firm that had represented the affairs of her father and grandfather before him) thought it foolhardy that the old woman should persist in the huge house when the land, the neighborhood, the very address was worth a small fortune (*better than no fortune at all*, he always added with a wink that had become so predictable it resembled a tic). Moreover, as administrator of Louisa's affairs, Mr Shillingcote knew that her will had not (as yet) designated an heir to the house and he entertained himself with the prospect that she would confer the house on him for his many years of service and courtesy, a panoply of possibility mentally performed by a huge cast of pounds and pence, operatically enriching his account. Louisa's co-worker at the Explorers' Club, Diana Dufour, thought that a woman living alone in such grand quarters was, quite simply, politically incorrect.

Diana Dufour had come to work at the Explorers' Club in 1958 when it had the rather grander name of The Society for Overseas Exploration, which was what it was called when Louisa went to work there as an indexer in 1946. That title too was a comedown from the Society for Imperial Exploration which was what it was called for its first 125 years. Whatever its designation, the Club was rather incongruously housed between legations and far more affluent associations in Belgrave Square, the quarters willed to the Club in 1878 by Sir William Barry, the famous Imperial Explorer. It sat in that graceful London square, proud but penniless, testifying with its neighbors to a more leisurely age, less uncertain times and lest its interior shabbiness be immediately apparent, the brass plate, the marble stairs were shined and swept daily by Mrs Jobson, the

Club's charwoman and bedmaker. Inside, however, and away from the prying eyes of those who might judge it harshly, the Club was dusty, dim, faded and tarnished; the heads and antlers, the glass eyes, the fangs and horns and tusks of animals shot in the course of Imperial Explorations (including the enormous upright polar bear in the foyer, his expression forever frozen into outrage) in fact were only cleaned and dusted once a year, in December, always close to Christmas.

'It's a dreadful waste of money,' Diana asserted of the animal cleaning as she stood negligently in the doorway of Louisa's small office with its glassed-in bookshelves and wooden filing cabinets and potted plants on the sill. Diana could stand negligently, but she could never be said to have lounged under any circumstances; she was a woman of large proportions and her political views were in keeping with her physical stature. 'Besides, the place smells of old wet hair for days after they've cleaned.'

'That's why we have it done close to Christmas,' Louisa replied as she continued jotting notes of the Index of Journals she maintained for the club. 'We only have to endure the smell for a day or two and then we're off for the holidays.'

Their conversation was punctuated by the sound of a crashing bucket, a male voice cursing and a female voice urging him to clean it up before it stained the parquet floor. Louisa closed up the journal from which she had copied the last entry in the table of contents and regarded the impassive clock, remarking casually on the hour, hoping that Diana would go back to her own cubicle.

Diana remained (as was her nature) impervious, commenting loudly on the ineptitude of the animal cleaners and adding in no uncertain terms that such clumsiness only underscored what the country had come to under Thatcher. Having elaborated on this theme, Diana then posed to Louisa the question she had asked each December 22 since 1958: would Louisa care to join her (and whatever leftish political group she was currently allied with) for Christmas Day? This year the Women's Anti-Nuke Coalition would hold a Christmas protest and –

'Thank you very much, Diana,' (Louisa had always given the same reply since 1958), 'but I'm sure my cousin Enid will invite me and as I've no other family but her, I shall probably spend the day with them.'

'You ought to think in terms of the Family of Man,' Diana counseled, preface to one of her speeches in which the Family of Man was depicted living happy, full, politically correct lives on the straight and narrow-gauge tracks laid out by Diana and her right-thinking leftish cohorts.

Louisa might have been afflicted with the entire speech, but Mr Shotworth appeared, advising the ladies that they might leave a little early today if they wished. Mr Shotworth was their superior and such was the shrunken grandeur of the Explorers' Club in these days of the shrunken globe, that these three, the pensioned porter, Mr (once Sergeant) Taft (who lost money on the horses) and the charwoman, Mrs Jobson (who lost money at the pub) were the only employees of an institution that had once boasted, required, four or five times that many people, whose halls had once rung with the hearty voices of adventuresome men. Mr Shotworth was a conscientious man of ongoingly indeterminate middle age whose good humor only failed him when he reflected at any length on the poverty and obscurity of the Explorers' Club, on its dwindling list of Trustees, on its meager prospects for the future. However, he

tried to remain always professional and even-tempered
at the Club, confining his bouts of unhappiness to his
home where he inflicted them on Mrs Shotworth who
told him many times she didn't deserve it and it wasn't
her fault.

Mr Shotworth was pulling on his gloves. 'Christmas
always creeps up on me,' he told Louisa and Diana,
'these last few years I'm scarcely aware of the season
until they come in to clean the –' his last word was lost in
the clang and scuffle of a falling ladder and a male voice
advising the animals to perform unnatural acts. Mr
Shotworth winced simultaneously at the crash and the
vulgarity. 'Well Miss Wyatt,' he continued bravely, 'my
wife and I are certainly looking forward to your Christmas Cordial again this year.'

'It's not mine, Mr Shotworth,' Louisa reminded him,
'It's Lady Aylesbury's.'

'Yes, but she is long dead –'

'More than two hundred years, I should think.'

'– And so the cordial might very properly be said to be
yours now. No one else makes it, do they?' (And to this
Louisa assented.) 'My wife says you should bottle up
your Christmas Cordial and sell it at Boots and make a
fortune.'

'I've no need of a fortune,' Louisa replied.

'Perhaps not, but the world could use such a cordial –
eh Miss Dufour? The Family of Man?'

'The remedies for the ills of our time are political,
economic and social,' Diana reminded him. 'They are
not to be found in a bottle, although,' she added, an
uncharacteristic gentleness softening her voice, 'if such
a thing could be done, it could be done only with
Louisa's Christmas Cordial, if it could be administered
to punks and plutocrats alike, then perhaps –' her tone
became almost dreamy before Diana recollected herself

[191]

and marched off (Diana always marched) to her own cubicle.

Mr Shotworth turned to Louisa and remarked, 'We used the last drop of our last year's Christmas Cordial in October, Miss Wyatt, and we, my wife and I, are sorely in need of the new bottle.' Mr Shotworth did not add that he had used the last drop of the cordial topically, applied it to his own throbbing head after Mrs Shotworth (fed up with his moping, morose mooning over the Explorers' Club) had flung the *Oxford Companion to English Literature* (old edition) at her husband, not really intending to hit him, only hoping that the thump of the book would rouse him from his (as she saw it) stupor. The *Oxford Companion*, however, had hit Mr Shotworth squarely in the temple and the repentant Mrs Shotworth had hastened to the kitchen cabinet where they kept the Christmas Cordial, taken the near-empty bottle and her own handkerchief and applied it to the bump rising on her husband's head, crooning – *Go ahead, Harry take the last swallow, dear, no don't let's look for the spoon, just drink it up, there's only a drop left and it will help you. It always has.* Kneeling together on their sitting-room floor, Mr and Mrs Shotworth shared the last swill of the Cordial, their arms around each other, her gray head on his shoulder, the warmth and equilibrium of their long marriage restored. Mr Shotworth however was not about to impart these dreary domestic circumstances to Miss Wyatt; to Miss Wyatt he said only that they had used the last of the Christmas Cordial when they felt the chill of autumn creeping over them, on a night when they both shivered and sniffled. 'We were perfectly fit the next day,' he concluded, considering that this was, in fact, the truth.

'"The vertues of this water are many,"' Louisa recited, chapter and verse from Lady Aylesbury's own notations, '"it comforteth, helpeth and preserveth. It balanceth the bile and the blood."'

Agreeing with this, Mr Shotworth went off humming 'The Holly and the Ivy', and Louisa closed up her cubicle. She met Diana again at the porter's desk where Mr Taft put down his racing paper and handed the ladies their coats, hats and scarves. Louisa sat down on the huge chair (upholstered in crocodile skin) in the shadow of the polar bear and pulled on her galoshes while Mr Taft bemoaned the paucity of explorers actually staying in the club this holiday season. Only three. Total.

'Perhaps the Explorers' Club is too exclusive,' Diana Dufour offered, 'Perhaps we ought to open our membership to the masses.'

Mr Taft was aghast at this. In his own way Mr Taft was the most consummate snob among them. He pointed out that the Explorers' Club had indulged in quite enough democracy by admitting scientists and anthropologists (who, in the opinion of Mr Taft were not explorers in any sense) and travel writers who were a dubious lot at best. Besides these individuals, the Club had extended membership to any and all blood relations (and descendants) of the Club's once illustrious founders. (This for the sake of securing money as much as anything else).

'It's a pity,' Louisa observed, 'that we can't charge the animals for residency.' She nodded toward Pip which was the incongruous name accorded the outraged polar bear for as long as anyone could remember. 'Or the ghosts,' she added, alluding to the long-held, perpetually dismissed and never-quite-laid-to-rest notion that the ghosts of those illustrious Imperial Explorers, Sir William Barry, Sir Clive Rackham and Sir Matthew Curtis (who had fired the fatal shot at Pip) lingered among the parquet and wainscoting in the library, rattled the cases of memorabilia lining the halls and uneasily tenanted the spartan rooms overhead. 'If we tithed the ghosts and animals,' Louisa added, 'our coffers would be very full indeed.'

Bidding good-night to Diana and Mr Taft, Louisa walked, as quickly as her three-quarters of a century would permit, across Hyde Park to Bayswater Road, there to await the Number 12 or the Number 88 bus. The Tube would have been faster of course, but she disliked the Tube; nearly fifty years after the fact, going down down down into the bowels of the city, deep into the Underground stations reminded Louisa inevitably of the Blitz, of the War with all its associations of loss and deprivation and things never being quite the same. Besides, she enjoyed riding the bus, always climbed the stairs to sit amongst the smokers and the cigarette butts, chose a window seat (when possible) from which to view the city. Though she had lived in London nearly all her life, Louisa Wyatt never tired of the city, particularly at Christmas time when she could watch from the top of the bus and feel herself enfolded into the general celebration, caught up in the throngs of shoppers and over-worked clerks, imaginatively pulled into shops, even the most modest of which twinkled with fairy lights and the windows draped in shiny ropes of tinsel, overhearing, if not exchanging, greetings of good cheer, tidings of comfort and joy piped in over scratchy loudspeakers, the caroling of the bells and voices punctuated by the happy ring of the cash register.

In this general, impersonal sense Louisa Wyatt kept Christmas. Personally she had not had a tree, so much as one fairy light, a sprig of mistletoe or holly for thirty years. Maybe more. What would be the point? An old woman on her own? Louisa Wyatt's observances of the season were solitary, singular rites performed over many weeks in her own kitchen where she every year made Lady Aylesbury's Christmas Cordial, bottled it up, corked it, tied the bottles with ribbons and gave them away to people whose lives touched her own. The list, sadly, had diminished over the years and now only included the people at the Explorers' Club, Mr Shillingcote, her cousin Enid, plus a bottle each for the milkman, the postman, the two dustmen and reserving always two bottles for herself (one to store and one to use if necessary) and perhaps a couple of extras because one never quite knew. Did one?

The brutal cold chilled Louisa's old bones clear through by the time she arrived at her own street in Holland Park where the windows of the houses around hers (all long since divided into flats) advertised the multiplicity of the many lives therein. The windows of Louisa's house that fronted the street contrasted sadly; they remained draped, closed, obscured, rimed in the winter with great loops of frost that testified to rooms unwarmed with human breath or bodies, lacking expiration, expectation and voices.

It was however, a lovely house, one of those fine old homes, spacious and high-ceilinged, suggestive of long-vanished comforts and conventions. The house would have looked splendid with a thorough cleaning, the sort of blasting they were doing all over London, using high-powered tools to scrape away the accumulations of hundreds of years of coal fires and woodsmoke, exhaust, the grit and granular accretions of time. Louisa, in any event, could not have afforded the expensive cleaning. A satisfactory annuity set up by her father, who had been a prosperous wine merchant in his day, allowed her to keep the house without quite maintaining it; whatever got broken, for the most part, stayed broken and Louisa simply lived around it. What little she could spare from the annuity, she lavished on the herb garden. Her paltry though regular pay from the Explorers' Club saw to the few necessities of her limited life.

She put her key in the lock and stepped into the imposing front hall, though she waited to remove her coat, gloves and galoshes till she came into the kitchen which, along with the bath, her own bedroom and the small back sitting-room were the only rooms Louisa lived in or visited at all. All four of these rooms were on the same floor and looked out over the herb garden at the back (and beyond the garden wall to a block of insufferably ugly flats put up after the War). She switched on the kettle, the cooker, the heater and the squat old radio, took off her outer garments, washed the ink from her hands and heated up the teapot before slicing bread and putting it in the toaster, opening a tin of beans and heating it (in the tin) for her supper. She put on an apron, however, as though she were about to undertake the cooking of a grand meal and surveyed the collection of cordial bottles lined upon the enormous kitchen table (left over, like the web-strewn bells above the sink that once connected kitchen lives to other lives). Her work stood before her and she took pleasure and pride in it: the bottles of Lady Aylesbury's Christmas Cordial, wanting only proper corks, labels and ribbons – Louisa's private rite of Christmas which reflected the singular passion of her solitary life.

The passion of Louisa Wyatt's life was old cookbooks, not of the tawdry Elizabeth Craig vintage, not even of the Mrs Beeton variety (though Louisa had nothing personally against Mrs Beeton and the nineteenth century) but ancient cookbooks, two and three hundred years old, sometimes older, which she bought when she could find (and afford them) and which she explored on forays to museums and libraries where she copied out the contents of these old books in the same laborious hand she donated to her indexing work at the Explorers' Club. In copying these ancient recipes, Louisa preserved their exact spelling and syntax, taking pleasure in the immediate transcribing, as well as the many rereadings she gave to her efforts. Each book, each recipe, each and every entry, written and read, opened for Louisa (each time) a door to the past, granted her entrance and egress into a long-vanished world she came to know intimately and vicariously. Indeed over the many years she indulged in this passion, Louisa came to know and understand the past as few other people did; her knowledge of sixteenth- and seventeenth-century diction, her careful research into the meanings of their terms, her understanding of their methods, ingredients and the beliefs that underlay cookery in the past made her an expert, though in a world shackled to the automatic toaster, the electric kettle, the microwave and the Magimix, no one valued her expertise, or even acknowledged it.

Like most people, Louisa Wyatt had stumbled on the passion of her life in her youth, her gorgeous, carefree days at Oxford in the Thirties when, as a student at Lady Margaret Hall, she had reveled through the streets with her chums, punted on the river, bicycled vast distances, shared latenight cocoa and confidences. One day, killing time in the august confines of the Bodleian Library, researching a very boring essay due on the dissolution of the monasteries (Louisa was reading history), she stumbled on an indexed listing for an ancient recipe book dating vaguely from the time of the dissolution of the monasteries. She wrote out a ticket and waited, watching the rain pelt the silvery windows and hammer the cobbles below, until from somewhere in the vast uncharted capillaries of the Bodleian, there was brought to her a book with thick vellum binding, hand sewn with thick luscious pages writ in the thin spidery scrawl of a long-dead hand. The days she spent with that book told her nothing of the dissolution of the monasteries, but volumes about the conduct of life. She learned the ways in which these lost people had lived and breathed and had their being, treated their chilblains and agues and fevers, their palsies and rheumatism, their poxes (small and large); she learned how they grappled with infertility and difficult births, how they wasted not and what they wanted for, the rites by which they marked the passing of seasons, how they stowed the summer against the winter's chill, bottled the blossom against the bare branch, how and what they stewed and 'rosted', poached and stuffed and laid in a 'pritty hott oven,' how they made 'syder' and ale and 'cockwater' and a 'surfit of poppies' and cowslip wine: in short, how real people in the visceral past spent their daily lives, how they kept their souls united to bodies which had long since turned to dust. It was a turning point in her life.

Of course, when she went to Oxford, Louisa had not expected to discover a passion for ancient cookbooks. Like most young women she expected to come upon a young man at Oxford who would become the passion of her life, or at the very least her husband. Such a man did not materialize and as the War loomed closer, her mother (who knew whereof she spoke by having three unmarried younger sisters, thanks to the casualties of the First War) advised Louisa to marry and to marry soon. Louisa confided to her mother that there was no particular man for whom she felt anything approaching passion or love, requited or otherwise. To this her mother replied that one could live without passion, but living without a husband was difficult and unpleasant. *Look at Aunt Tilda, Aunt Charlotte and Aunt Jane living out their days in cramped poverty in Ilfracombe, twittering over eiderdowns and hot-water bottles and cheese rinds*. Louisa's mother contrasted this grim picture of the aunts' life wordlessly with her own comfortable connubial existence in Holland Park. Louisa's mother added sagely that she should marry a young man now; after the war there would not be any young men. There might be survivors, but they would no longer be young.

In this, as in nearly everything else, her mother was correct. More correct than she could have known. Both Louisa's brothers died in the War, one in Burma and one in the North African campaign; towards the end of the War her sister married a Yank and moved with him to Arizona, never to return to England. Alone of her siblings, Louisa remained in the Holland Park house, her thirties looming before her and no husband in sight. She accepted the lack of a husband (certainly her fate was shared by many other women of her generation), but it seemed to Louisa unfair that her moral, upright upbringing should never have been tested beyond a moonlit kiss at the college gate in the spring of 1937. Like other women, she had expected that love (and a lover) would make a fore-ordained stop in her life, rather like a train one waits for on a crowded platform for a long time, till the crowd thins out and one waits alone.

As she passed through her thirties, Louisa found herself – gradually, guiltily, furtively and certainly not intending to tell definite lies – making up a lover: a man compounded of the might-have-beens, a man who, though he lacked substance, eventually came into a name. *Julian*. Julian seemed a good sort of name for one's lost lover – a musical, evocative name with a dash of the stately. She began alluding casually and in glib conversations with strangers to 'Julian' and over the years the allusions coalesced into anecdotes that highlighted Julian's David Niven wit, his Leslie Howard charm, his cleverness and thoughtfulness and how he had died in the War. Since everyone had someone who had died in the War, she was accorded a measure of patriotic sympathy that also tended to give Julian, as it were, weight and girth. Moreover, as the people closest to her (those aforementioned friends and family who thought Louisa ought to have 'done something' with her life) died off, Julian's vivacity (so to speak) increased commensurately. Diana Dufour knew the story of Louisa's passionate love affair with poor Julian who had died early in the War. (Dunkirk, in fact.) Mr Shotworth knew the story of Julian, as did Mr Taft and Mrs Jobson. Louisa's cousin Enid never questioned the existence of Julian, nor did Mr Shillingcote. How could they? On those rare occasions when they came to call at the Holland Park house, they saw Julian's picture on the mantel of the small back sitting-room, amongst the gallery of other framed family photographs. At first Louisa had put Julian's picture at the back of the gallery, inching him forward, year by year, till he now occupied a central situation: the hub, if not the husband.

Louisa had stumbled on Julian's picture one memorable day in the spring of 1957 when she had gone up to Oxford (this in the days when she drove and had a car) to further research old cookbooks at the Bodleian. On Saturday the library closed at noon and as it was the first bright day of the daffodil spring, she decided to drive to Woodstock before returning to London, perhaps to have a walk around the grounds of Blenheim Palace and a look in Featherstone's Rare Books. Featherstone very often had old cookbooks in his dusty collections and in fact he sometimes kept the really ancient ones aside for her, knowing that every few weeks in good weather, she came up to Oxford.

She was alarmed that spring day in 1957 to drive into Woodstock and discover that Featherstone's Rare Books sported a new sign: YE SPINNING WHEEL: *Antiques and Rare Books*. Mr Featherstone was rather shamefaced about the change, but launched into a long catalog of causes (mostly having to do with tourists) that had brought him to this effect. As he was talking, Louisa's eye fell on a silver-framed photograph. The frame was for sale. Very expensive – but then Mr Featherstone added, noting that Miss Wyatt's eyes were riveted to it – it was after all sterling silver and very old and look at the workmanship and –

'That's not an old photograph in it,' Louisa observed.

Mr Featherstone put on his glasses and regarded it more closely. 'Rather old', he remarked optimistically, 'but it's the frame, Miss Wyatt, just lift that frame and you'll see –'

Louisa did lift the frame, but the opulence and intricacy of the worked silver was not what had arrested her attention or held it now. Inside was a photograph (neither quite snapshot nor quite studio portrait) of a man without any background visible behind him, a young man, well-dressed in the style of the Thirties, with thick unruly dark hair. He was smiling and the expression on his face, the eyes, the jaunty style of the shoulder suggested the wit of David Niven, the dash of Leslie Howard, good manners, good morals, good upbringing combined with irresistible impertinence and cheer. Dark eyes, dark hair, fair skin, the man was saved from conventional cosmetic beauty by his mouth: a shade too small for beauty. Clearly and without doubt: this was Julian. 'Who is the person in this picture?' Louisa inquired affably, still hefting the frame and pretending to be impressed with its every sterling quality.

Mr Featherstone shrugged. The frame, photo included, had come with a huge consignment from some warehouse or another, crate after crate of goods from a number of estates all puddled and muddled together in catalogs on which Mr Featherstone had successfully bid, though he could remember no particulars on any of it because, as he reminded Louisa, he was new at the antique business, but he assured her none the less that he did remember they were very old families and very old estates and he waxed on at some length about nothing being the same since the War, hard times, and all the great estates breaking up, its being rather akin to the dissolution of the monasteries and so on and then he added that she could certainly take the picture out, that he had only left it in because it showed the frame off to good advantage.

'That won't be necessary,' said Louisa, plunking down her chequebook and uncapping her pen.

'Don't you want to have a look at the cookbooks, Miss Wyatt?' Mr Featherstone inquired. 'I've got one very old one, hand-written in fact, that I've been saving for you.'

'That's very good of you, Mr Featherstone.'

'I should tell you though, it's very expensive.' (And seeing that she was in a spendthrift mood and the book was not yet marked with a price, it instantly became more expensive yet; if she balked, he could always bring the price down. Just for her.)

Louisa did not balk. She paid. She would have paid twice that for the photograph of her dead lover, Julian, and for the hand-written cookbook of Anne, Lady

Aylesbury who, from that day forward, became, in a manner of speaking, Louisa Wyatt's best friend.

At first Louisa enthusiastically approached dreary genealogical libraries trying to dig up information on Anne, Lady Aylesbury, but it was difficult going, confusing and unrewarding. By the summer of 1957 she had given it up altogether and, in a cavalier fashion, decided to take Lady Aylesbury at her word, that is, the words so beautifully transcribed in the hand-sewn cookbook, written in a hand so elegant, so clear, it seemed to have the ring of a flawless soprano. This imaginative approach to Lady Aylesbury seemed the better part of valor and Louisa spent the long evenings that summer in her overgrown garden reading and rereading the cookbook carefully divided into *Cookery, Sweetmeats and Remedies*, the recipe for the Christmas Cordial granted its own singular place on a leaf of paper between *Sweetmeats and Remedies*. Bringing her expertise to bear on the internal evidence, Louisa surmised that Anne, Lady Aylesbury had been married, the mistress of a vast household and the mother of many children. (This latter conclusion drawn from listings of sovereign remedies for childhood afflictions, the sheer number of which further suggested that Lady Aylesbury might have seen a good many children to the grave.) Clearly Lady Aylesbury was a consummate gardener – this fact supported by the intricate and elaborate herb garden Lady Aylesbury laid out at the back of the book with space for nearly every herb that would grow in Northern Europe (and some that would not). Louisa began, that very summer, to lay out her own herb garden, hiring men to do the initial difficult digging, pulling up and tearing out and then planting everything herself according to Lady Aylesbury's design, albeit in a diminished and not altogether successful fashion.

Louisa's expertise further allowed her to estimate that Anne, Lady Aylesbury had lived in the mid-eighteenth century and Louisa's twenty years of poring over ancient cookbooks enabled her to date some of the recipes from much earlier eras, Stuart England, Elizabethan, Tudor, some recipes even wafting the odors (rosewater, saffron, and almond milk) of the Middle Ages. The presence of these earlier recipes indicated that Lady Aylesbury's family was a very old one, a family that had managed to maintain its lands and superiority over hundreds of years. Louisa further deduced that the family was enormously wealthy, given the luxuries prodigally lavished throughout: the currants and cloves and pomegranates, butter and sugar and dates, the nutmeg, ginger, musk and ambergris, Seville oranges and lemons, olives, capers and a cornucopian number of vegetables to be sauced, tansied, tarted, put into pastry 'coffins' and used in 'sallets'. The grandeur, expense, expanse, the lavish generosity everywhere abundant in the cookbook conjured in Louisa's mind a sprawling manor with opulent gardens where even in winter the smell of boxwood floated on the fogs and crackling fires warmed every room in Lady Aylesbury's grand house. At Christmastime Louisa pictured prickly holly protruding from huge vases set on inlaid tables in each bedroom and along the portrait-lined halls. The drawing-room, hung with yellow damask and satin curtains the color of caramel, would boast a harpsichord, a harp and violin before the ten-foot windows. The dining-room at Christmas would be warmed by charcoal braziers and lit by a million vanilla-colored candles strewing golden light on Lady Aylesbury (beaming at the top of the long polished table) and all her guests: portly, well-fed, wigged and waistcoated men taking snuff, and women in satin sniffing pomander balls, young men, perhaps impecunious younger sons, paying court to marriageable young women with dowries and doting Papas, married women flirting with gusto and impunity, heavy-breasted dowagers, their white hair further powdered white, casting knowing glances on all these goings-on while they all feasted on pastries and peacock, on legs of lamb stuffed with sweetmeats and sparrows stewed with oranges, on tansies and syllabubs and marchpane cakes and all of it washed down with 'ye best gascoyne wine,' the whole gorgeous edifice supported by a bevy of eager, well-cared-for servants: thumping good-natured wenches and blustering boys, cooks who wielded ladles with the authority of scepters, ruddy men who smelled of straw and leather stamping their cold feet by the roaring kitchen fire, servants in livery darting up and down the stairs, laden with trays and silver serving-dishes, stone-faced before the gentry, amiable over a fireside flagon of ale once their duties finished.

All this – memory and imagination – along with twenty-five different herbs and spices laid up in faire water, steeped over days then dried and bruised and shredded and added to ye best gascoyne wine to be distilled finally into the Christmas Cordial Louisa made up each year from Lady Aylesbury's recipe, which was complete with a long list of the 'vertues of this water'. And when Louisa gave the cordial as gifts to her friends, the hundreds of years between herself and Lady Aylesbury seemed to contract with a snap and she saw herself in the same beautiful, bountiful light and imagined that Lady Aylesbury too had offered the Christmas Cordials to each individual, not only as a token of the season, but assuring them of her recognition of their unique qualities, her understanding of their secret hurts and ills, comforting them with whispered promises of the cordial's efficacy against whatever ailed their bodies, whatever unhappiness unbalanced their minds, whatever loss or hope denied troubled their hearts.

Louisa pulled the tin of beans off the cooker and burnt her fingers in the process. She sucked on the burnt fingers of the one hand while, with the other, she dumped the beans over the slice of toast on a plastic plate. She was about to eat them when the doorbell rang and she mentioned (to no one in particular) that it was probably Enid. She took off her apron and went to the door.

It was Enid with the youngest of her brood in tow, a girl. 'How good to see you, Enid,' cried Louisa, genuinely happy to have her intuitions validated (and they so frequently were that they ceased to be intuitions and came to be expectations).

Louisa led her guests down the cold hall to the back sitting-room where she flicked on the electric fire and gave a secret, connubial smile to Julian (who in their years together had become as much husband as lover) and remarked to Enid how Margot had grown.

'No, Louisa, this is Molly. My youngest. Margot is the –'

'Of course. How stupid of me. Let me get you a cup of tea, Enid. It will take the chill off you till the room warms up.'

'No, thank you just the same, Louisa, I must get back. Jack expects his supper. Molly and I were just on our way home from some shopping and we thought we would stop in and invite you for Christmas instead of ringing you on the phone. Please do come Christmas Day – unless you've another invitation.' Enid always offered this last caveat with some trepidation, fearful lest someone else might have wormed their way into Louisa's affections, to say nothing of the possibilities of her last will and testament. Moreover, Enid never phoned with the Christmas invitation, but always delivered it in person so that she might see the house she hoped to inherit.

Enid (bundled up, wearing beneath her shabby coat the moth-brown cardigan Louisa imagined her to have been born in some forty-five years before) sat down on the sofa with her daughter. The girl was about twelve, entering into the gangly cocoon of adolescence from which she would emerge a plain young woman. All Enid's children were plain, though when they were little Enid believed them to be winsome moppets, but as they grew up, even Enid had to admit that they had inherited her own air of nervous desperation and their father's shambling sloth. Still, Enid eternally hoped that one of the children might kindle affection in her cousin's childless breast and so assuredly secure the house for the family when the old lady passed on – which she showed no inclination to do, and Enid could not help but wince every time Louisa remarked that her Aunt Charlotte had lived to be ninety. 'Your garden's looking very ghostly this time of year,' Enid remarked with a glance out the velvet-curtained window. (Resolving inwardly that when she inherited the house, down would come those ghastly green velvet curtains.)

'All gardens look ghostly this time of year – it's the frost and ice on all the cobwebs, don't you think? Makes the plants look bearded and hoary, especially with everything droopy and frost-bitten, reminds you of a graveyard and a skeleton's toothless smile.'

'Hmmm,' replied Enid whose powers of imagination were easily taxed. Hmmm managed to sound both neutral and positive at the same moment.

'But my herbs did rather well this summer and I think the Christmas Cordial will be especially good.'

'Hmmm.'

'In fact I feel certain Jack will find the Christmas Cordial especially helpful this year. Still suffers from Troubled Tummy, does he?'

Enid smiled wanly, unwilling to discuss her dyspeptic (and consequently surly) husband.

'"The vertues of this water are good against the bloat of ye bellye and the winds of flatulence,"' Louisa quoted from Lady Aylesbury who (lady though she was) did not shrink from being physiologically precise. '"It helpeth the wamblings and gripings of the bellye and killeth the worms in ye body."'

'Yes,' replied Enid, 'We've used our last year's cordial all up. By August,' she added, hoping to flatter her cousin. In fact Jack (he of wambling griping bellye, propelled by the winds of flatulence) not only would not touch the stuff, but instructed his wife to chuck it out on Boxing Day. Enid could not bring herself to defy her husband, but neither could she obey him. She had twenty-five bottles of Christmas Cordial stuffed at the back of the cupboard in her one and only bathroom, kept there (when the space was so much wanted for other things) in the superstitious belief that they amounted to a kind of account. For Enid, to hear one of these bottles break would break her heart, like the smashing of her every hope. Nibbling on her fingernails, Enid lied ably. 'The Christmas Cordial has been very good for Jack's dyspepsia, Louisa. He's said so. Many times.'

Molly gave her mother a sneer of wonderment and was about to lisp some cute morsel of childish truth when her mother gouged her in the ribs and admonished her not to fidget. 'Molly, show your Aunt Louisa',

(Enid instructed the children to call her Aunt Louisa hoping to call forth maternal feeling from those unused breasts) 'your new orthodontic work.'

Molly bared a mouth full of metal in an expression that reminded Louisa of Pip the polar bear. Louisa remarked the equivalent of How Nice Dear while Molly and Enid waxed on in virtual unison about the intricacies of orthodontic work. Louisa reminded them (without a flicker of a smile) that according to Lady Aylesbury, the Christmas Cordial also 'helpeth the stinking breath' which effectively closed the subject.

Enid rose. 'Shall we look for you, then, Louisa, Christmas Day?'

'Thank you very much. Yes, of course.' Louisa was grateful for the invitation (since it spared her the Women's Anti-Nuke Coalition), but she did not look forward to a meal with the flatulent Jack. 'You're the closest thing I have to family, Enid,' she added.

Enid's whole face lit, her fatigue and pinched desperation easing under the glow, the way a candle illuminates frost crystallized on a frozen pane.

'Shall I bring anything?'

'Oh, you needn't, Louisa. Just the Christmas Cordial.' When her children were little Enid relished the dream that Louisa would come with a good deal more than a bottle of Christmas Cordial, hoping Louisa (whom she thought to be rich) would arrive in Shepherd's Bush laden with beribboned, bright-wrapped parcels of toys to delight the moppets. Enid saw Louisa as a female Scrooge and cast her own family as the Cratchits, though she mercifully had no lame children and her husband Jack could not, by the remotest stretch of the imagination, pass for the good-natured Bob

Cratchit; and besides, as her little children grew up into dispirited youths, the vision paled, staled and crumbled, leaving Enid with no fodder for her starved imagination, save for the hope of inheriting the Holland Park House. 'We really ought to get together more often than just at Christmas,' Enid offered shyly. 'Being family and all.'

Louisa, who knew full well her cousin's limited life with the constantly cross Jack and who sympathized with her hopes for the Holland Park house (knowing, too, it would not make the least difference to Jack), was touched by Enid's offer. She put her thin arm around Enid and squeezed her. 'Isn't it amazing how time gets away from you?'

'Yes,' Enid concurred, smiling and feeling altogether better than when she'd arrived, as she and the heavy-metal Molly stepped outside into the lamplit dark with many wishes for the season and sage observations on the brutal cold.

After they left, Louisa turned off the electric fire in the sitting-room and hurried back into the warm kitchen. The beans and toast were cold, as was her tea. She made a fresh pot of hot tea, but ate the beans and toast as they were. Food, that is the food she actually ate, mattered little to Louisa and reheating the beans would be too much trouble to take for herself. As she ate her solitary meal to the tune of Christmas carols on the radio, she reflected that if Julian had lived, everything would have been different; they would have had lovely meals and Louisa's reputation as a great cook gone far and wide amongst their many friends; she would have been renowned for gala dinner parties, daringly traditional, each one gleaming for years ever after in the minds of her guests. She often sat up late at night reading ancient cookbooks in bed and fell asleep dreaming of the meals she might have made for Julian, their children, their many friends, these feasts mingling with Lady Aylesbury's: all the guests, eighteenth-century and contemporary alike, arriving with relish and good cheer and leaving surfeited with excellent food, brilliant hospitality, bright wines, bonny ports, glowing sherries, taking their leave in moments imbued with conviviality, affection and memory.

Louisa Wyatt read cookbooks the way other women read novels; she kept them by her bed and in a basket in the bathroom equidistant (and easily reachable) from either the tub or the toilet. For Louisa these well-known recipes had the vivacity of characters from a much-loved novel, people one could go back to again and again, savoring their noble lives, pitying their squandered loves, weeping for their renounced affections, rejoicing when their passions and principles were rewarded, enjoying, over and over, all those gambles that may be safely taken on paper but not in life. Lady Aylesbury was the foremost of Louisa's heroines and she had fallen into the habit of chatting with her night after night: talk between equals (while Louisa ate cold beans on toast) of 'How to Make a Lettis Tarte' and the techniques needed to perfect 'A Capon Roste with Oysters', the amenities of 'A Gruelle of French Barley' (which they agreed would stir the invalid's wan appetite), discussion between experts of the intricacies of Rice Florentine, the art of fritters and frumenty, of possets and fools and cheesecakes and syllabubs and (oh, can you imagine!) 'A Creme Made of Fresh Snowe.' While Louisa fortified her body with cold beans on toast, she fortified her imagination with Lady Aylesbury's cookbook and the multitude of dishes that she made from it, dishes she served to Julian and the children they might have had and, indeed, to the grandchildren they might have had, all of whom Louisa imagined as golden-haired moppets; eager, bouncing girls and shy, serious little boys, or sometimes, as suited her fancy, she imagined them as beautiful young men and women about to go up to Oxford, to embark on lives of wonder and achievement, passion and requited love. She never imagined them any older than that. She could not bear to.

The next day she waited, teeth chattering in the front hall, for the post to come through the slot and then stuck her head out and asked the postman about the weather.

'It ain't a day for man nor beast, Miss Wyatt,' he replied, clapping his cold hands together and inwardly cursing the bleeding cold. He was a dim, fraying man of about forty with a wreath of graying hair around a bald head which he always kept covered with his hat. 'It ain't a day for you to go out.'

'Oh, I must go out today. The Club has its Christmas party.'

The postman hadn't any idea what sort of Club she might be referring to, guessing it to be a bridge club or knitting party, something of that sort, and because of the cold, didn't stop to inquire. 'Have another bottle of that Christmas Cordial, do you, Miss Wyatt?'

'Tomorrow,' she assured him.

'You can't buy a better remedy for the bunions.' He pointed to his feet and shook his head. 'Looking forward to it, I am,' he added with a grin and a wave, not admitting that he had squandered his last year's bottle in June when his wife had left him.

When it was time to go to work, Louisa took the postman at his word and indulged in the unwonted luxury of calling a cab. She could not risk dropping the box full of Christmas Cordials. She directed the cabby to the Explorers' Club in Belgrave Square, hoping he might think she was an explorer and not a mere indexer of journal articles for more than forty years.

They arrived at the Club and the cabby (a young man with a total of five gold rings in his ears) hopped out and opened the door for her, held her ancient arm up the marble steps and then went back to the chugging car to get the box, wadded with newspaper, in which she carried the bottles of Christmas Cordial to be given to the staff. Always on the day before Christmas Eve, she, Diana Dufour, Mr Shotworth, Mr Taft and Mrs Jobson celebrated the season in the Captain Cook Library and notes were put into the boxes of any guests at the Club who might wish to join them. Inevitably these guests were men whose inclination to explore and habits of travel had denied them the pleasures (and pangs) of family, and they were usually grateful for the invitation and joined the staff for a sip of sweet wine, a bite of cake and a bit of Christmas cheer.

The newly-cleaned animal heads dotting the walls of the Captain Cook Library still stank of wet hair, but the fire was cheerful and the room almost warm and certainly pleasant when they assembled that afternoon, the staff and the three Club guests: Colonel Stanhope who was associated in some way with Africa, Mr Thrumley whose connection with the Club was of long standing, having done something wonderful (no one could quite remember what) in the days of the Raj, and Mr Turner, an American travel writer who was between travels (and between advances from his publisher) and who, as he explained to Louisa, was staying in London awhile to recover completely from jet lag.

Louisa remarked to Mr Turner, (as she did to all Americans with whom she chanced to come in contact), that she felt a special affinity for Americans, that her sister had married an American at the end of the War

[213]

and moved to Arizona, 'which I imagine must be something like Egypt,' she added, 'without the pyramids.'

Mr Turner had been to both Arizona and Egypt, discoursed a good while on the Nile being rather like the Colorado River and then turned the conversation back to his jet lag. Seasoned and experienced traveler that he was (he informed Miss Wyatt), jet lag never much bothered him in the past, but lately it seemed to attack him and he suffered grievously, inexplicably. He was a man of about fifty (Louisa reckoned as she nodded her white frizzy head and sipped her sweet wine) who must have recently made the dreadful discovery that his body was beginning to echo with the muffled creaks and cranks of age, who had recently recognized that a half-century had passed over or around or beneath him, that his past was irrevocably gone, his continuing future no longer assured and his present a good deal less pleasant than it had been prior to this baleful illumination. 'I find the jet lag affects more than my body,' Mr Turner confessed. 'It gets to my mind. Lately it just undoes me. I get depressed and forgetful,' he added with a contradictory laugh, 'and these are things no traveler can afford.' He laughed again to further trivialize the discussion and quoted from one of his own books, '"Depression is a luxury no traveler can afford. It is *not* in the budget!"'

'Melancholia, would you say?' inquired Louisa.

He shook his head somberly. 'Clinical depression. That's what my doctor in America says. He gave me a prescription to treat clinical depression.'

'You must fly through a good many time zones,' she observed inconsequentially, listening with one ear as Diana's voice grew shrill in her efforts to convert those two old servants of the Empire, Colonel Stanhope and Mr Thrumley, to her views regarding the Family of Mankind.

'To pass through time zones is part of the traveler's package and privilege. It's just that I find I can't take it like I used to,' Mr Turner added glumly.

'I've never been out of England myself.' Louisa returned her attention to the American. 'I could have traveled, I suppose, after Oxford, but the War came along and after the War – well, everything was different and I can't remember just now why I didn't travel, but I didn't. And of course now, at my advanced age, the opportunity's passed me by altogether, hasn't it?'

'Advanced age?' Mr Turner inquired gallantly. 'You don't look a day over sixty.'

At this Louisa revised her initial sour impression of the man. 'Perhaps I can help you,' she offered as she led him to the library table where the box of cordials sat. She always brought a few extra bottles with her each year so that Club guests (if they wanted a bottle) should not feel excluded. 'Every year I make a Christmas Cordial from an ancient recipe,' she explained to him. 'I follow it exactly. The book I got it from was transcribed by a beautiful hand in the eighteenth century, but the cordial, I know, is a good deal older than that and I feel certain this cordial has been helping hundreds of people for hundreds of years.' She smiled at him reassuringly. 'Take it sparingly, Mr Turner. A scant teaspoon at a time, I should think. No more. "The vertues of this water are many, it comforteth the vital spirits. It draweth away melancholy, lethargie and the phlegm. It comforteth against the ague and wardeth off all plagues and pestilences," and though Lady Aylesbury says nothing about jet lag, I'm certain it can help that too. "It restoreth the humours, and whosoever shall drink of this water, it preserveth their health and causeth them to look young."'

'Did you make all of that up?' he asked, abashed.

'I'm reciting. Quoting from the cookbook.'

'I see Miss Wyatt has offered you one of her famous Christmas Cordials,' Mr Shotworth interrupted them genially. In these Christmas gatherings Mr Shotworth's best nature bloomed; he made himself personally responsible for the cheer and comfort of everyone, from Mrs Jobson to Colonel Stanhope. 'You are a lucky man, Mr Turner.'

'I am?'

'Oh yes, I can attest personally to the efficacy of Miss Wyatt's Christmas Cordial. It does everything she says it does.'

'It's not mine, Mr Shotworth,' she corrected him. 'It's Lady Aylesbury's.'

'A family recipe?' inquired Mr Turner.

'In a manner of speaking,' Louisa replied confidently. (After all, she had met Lady Aylesbury the same day she met Julian.)

'I don't doubt that you're skeptical, Mr Turner,' Mr Shotworth continued, 'but we here at the Club, we swear by it. My wife always tries a shot of the Christmas Cordial before she takes so much as an aspirin,' he added truthfully.

Mrs Jobson, after discreetly filling her wine glass once again, joined them at the library table, adding her praise. 'I give the Christmas Cordial to my daughter when she started her – you know – and it worked. She takes a scant sip every month. So do I. What is it they're calling that these days – PMS, yes? Well, a sip of Miss Wyatt's Christmas Cordial and it's PMS – goodbye!' she added with a yellow-toothed grin. Mrs Jobson was a woman in her late thirties, perhaps overfond of the bottle, but understandably so; she was either widowed or divorced, certainly the deserted mother of three children whom she had raised alone for ten years, and the staff's pity for her was absolutely unanimous after her eldest boy once came to the Club to ask her for money; he had a bright green mohawk and a bullet shell hanging from a ring in his ear. Whatever Mrs Jobson's fondness for the bottle, she had never in ten years missed a day of work due to hangover and while she might have shared the woes of her menstrual cycle with the assembled company, she did not deign to add that she had also used the Christmas Cordial successfully against the hangovers which had crippled her in the old days. 'A tonic, sir!' Mrs Jobson addressed Mr Turner authoritatively, 'that's what this 'ere Christmas Cordial is. No mistaking. Why, Miss Wyatt might've been a rich woman if she'd bottled it up, but it's better like this, if you know what I mean.' (Clearly Mr Turner did not.) 'I mean, it's more exclusive, like, makes you feel you've got something special, like you've something all your own to cure whatever ails you and no one else.' She regarded the bottles lovingly. 'Is it the ailing makes you call it Lady Aylesbury's, Miss Wyatt?'

'No. That was the name of the woman who wrote the recipes in the book.'

Mrs Jobson again turned to Mr Turner, 'Well, sir, whatever's got at you, the pain in the gut, palsy in the hand, the bad bowels, you can take it from me, you can, the Christmas Cordial is the very ticket. The very one, Mr . . . Mr . . .'

'Turner,' replied the American, annoyed at having his innards discussed. Clinical depression. Jet lag. That's what he had in mind.

Mrs Jobson wandered away to refill her glass yet again and get the last bit of cake. She took a roundabout route to avoid Diana, Colonel Stanhope and Mr Thrumley whose discussion had escalated (and their voices correspondingly elevated) to the rights of individuals versus the rights of nations, the argument gath-

[217]

ering such verve and acrimony that even Diana glanced wishfully at the library table with its bright beribboned bottles of Christmas Cordial.

Mr Taft put down his wine glass, bid adieu and Happy Christmas to Mrs Jobson, and ambled in his military fashion over to the library table to say his goodbyes and wish them all the best of the season. Louisa gave him his bottle and in accepting it, Mr Taft's blue eyes sparkled and he turned to the American (whose name he remembered as that was part of his job, the careful remembering of names). 'Now Mr Turner, I don't know what Miss Wyatt puts in her cordial, sir, but I'd swear it was a bit of the season itself. Whenever I've lost at the ponies or my luck's run down or the old war wound,' (he patted his thigh affectionately) 'acts up, I take a bit of this and – I can't explain it, sir – but it brightens me right up. My old lady, my wife, Mr Turner, I think she hit on it. Bertie – the wife says to me – Bertie, that Miss Wyatt's cordial, it's like a nip of Christmas – whenever you need it during the year. Any old time. You can just close your eyes, Bertie, drop a teaspoon of this down your gullet and hear "The Holly and the Ivy" singing in your veins.'

'The Holly and the Ivy' was on Louisa's lips as she put the key in her lock, closed the door behind her and hastened down the passage to the kitchen where she remained shivering, bundled until the cooker and kettle and heater had all warmed up. Despite the cold, she was in a cheerful holiday mood, full of gratitude and affection for her friends at the Explorers' Club, convinced that no other job could have afforded her such friends and such pleasures – to say nothing of allowing her to continue working part time long past retirement age. Then she laughed out loud to think of Diana Dufour and the two old servants of the Empire, Mr Thrumley and Colonel Stanhope. 'Oh, you should have seen it,' she said to no one in particular (as there was no one there), 'Diana had poor Mr Thrumley by the lapels! Diana the huntress indeed! That girl ought to have run for Parliament,' she remarked, knowing full well that thirty years stood between Diana and any girlhood she might have enjoyed. As the warmth percolated through the kitchen, Louisa's account of the afternoon's festivities grew more animated and precise, as though reconstructing the event for the entertainment of someone intimately involved, but who could not have been at the Club, someone whose presence seemed to gather without quite coalescing, to dissipate without quite disappearing. 'And Colonel Stanhope, when I gave him his bottle of the Cordial, he called me *dear lady* and said I should have labeled the Cordial, 'Spirits of Christmas'. And well, naturally I told him it was *your* cordial, the recipe in your own hand, my dear, of course. And, did you remember we'd given Colonel Stanhope a bottle the Christmas of 1973? Neither did I, but Colonel Stanhope did. Oh yes, and he told everyone there that he'd taken the bottle with him to Angola and that the Christmas Cordial – and that alone – had got him through the war. No, I don't know which war. People like Colonel Stanhope are always getting through one war or another, aren't they? Yes, of course I'm hurrying. I haven't forgotten Mr Shillingcote's coming to tea. One cannot forget Mr Shillingcote, can one?' And then Louisa bit back a smile and silently concurred that one wasn't allowed to. She surveyed her tray: teapot, cups, saucers, milk, sugar, a plate of shop-bought vanilla biscuits, (shop-bought so long ago they looked to have been cut from stucco). She was in the midst of relating the woes of Mr Turner, the American travel writer, when the doorbell rang. 'Clinical depression indeed!' she concluded with a sniff. 'Melancholia, that's what ails Mr Turner and of course the virtues of the cordial will –'

The bell rang again. Mr Shillingcote, for all his *bonhomie*, was not a man to be kept waiting but a man for whom time was money, and he treated both with equal respect. Indeed, in bestowing his time upon Louisa Wyatt, he considered himself to be giving her a gift that could not be ribboned or wrapped.

After the usual pleasantries in the freezing front hall, Louisa led him to the frosty back sitting-room where she flicked on the electric fire, chagrined not to have done so earlier. Mr Shillingcote commented on the cold, adding, 'Tis the season to be jolly,' to which Louisa, in her cracked contralto, sang the refrain and told him the tea would be ready directly.

Mr Shillingcote thanked her and lowered himself to the couch. He had the big, ramshackle frame of an athletic schoolboy whose prowess had gone lumpy in all the predictable places. He had a long horsey face and a thick mane of hair that was once blonde, but turning gray now and coarsening in the process. 'I'm hoping you'll join us on Christmas Day, Louisa.' He always took this informal line with her, though his predecessor had never called her anything but Miss Wyatt. 'My wife is making a tremendous Christmas pudding from a recipe that's been in her family since the days of Queen Victoria.'

'That's hardly long ago at all, is it?'

'Long enough, I should think!' he replied, taking offense at the implied rebuff to the dignity of his wife's family.

'I only meant that when you think of it, I was born not so very long after Victoria died.'

'Were you at that?' cried Mr Shillingcote, knowing full well what year Louisa Wyatt was born in and guessing constantly (and against his better nature) what year she might die in, which brought him round to his favorite subject. 'Yes, this old house must have been grand in those days.'

'Comfortable, Mr Shillingcote. Hardly grand. Not, certainly of the order of Lady Aylesbury's.'

The solicitor colored slightly. 'Well, I'm sure this house would have some tales to tell if the walls could talk.'

'Do you think so?' Louisa glanced at the green velvet curtains, the fraying furniture, the stolid television (c. 1961), the boxy radio (c. 1948), the doilies and antimacassars and table runners and china dogs that still testified to her mother's fastidiousness. 'I rather doubt it. It's a staid old house, I should think. No ghosts whatever – certainly none in all the years I've lived here. There weren't any scandals in our family and –'

'I never meant to imply –'

'– of course not. I mean, my brothers both died very young and my sister went off to America and my mother and father were a very ordinary, upstanding sort of people and so, I believe, were the family previous to ours and no doubt, the family previous to that. I rather wish there were ghosts, and sometimes I like to think that miscreant merrymakers from the old Holland House, you know, the one that was bombed during the War and then demolished, might have reveled on these grounds and left some morsel of their youth and gaiety. I like to think of recklessly extravagant young men cavorting with young women who had been married off to husbands too old for them, committing adultery and being very much in love and –' Louisa smiled primly, aware, from the look on Mr Shillingcote's face, that she had said too much. 'Well, ghosts are unreliable at best, aren't they, Mr Shillingcote? Life is far more comfortable without them. What if one had a weepy, morose ghost, some Roundhead from the Civil War or a displaced priest bemoaning the dissolution of the monasteries?' Behind closed lips, Louisa put her tongue between her teeth and bit down hard, resolving not to let up till Mr Shillingcote spoke and not go on in that vein in any event.

'Of course one would prefer ghosts of one's own class and religion,' he offered drily and to this Louisa nodded, still biting her tongue. He went on in a lighter fashion, 'Perhaps it's just as well then that there are no ghosts, Louisa. That way, when they tear the place down, there won't be anyone chucked into the street!' He laughed in his horsey way.

'I don't intend to sell,' she reminded him.

He gestured broadly about the room. 'But really, Louisa – keeping all this up, why, it must ruin you!'

'I don't keep it up, Mr Shillingcote. You know very well that I only use these few rooms and all the rest of the house is sheeted and cold and I never have any cause to go upstairs.'

'Surely you'd be more comfortable in a cosy little flat? Certainly you'd be warmer,' he added with a glance to the electric fire whose glow had not yet permeated the sitting-room.

'I shan't be moving anywhere. Cosy or not. This is my home.'

Seeing that he had once again suffered his annual defeat, Mr Shillingcote took it manfully like the good sport he was and after making his customary remark about a small fortune being better than no fortune at all, he contradicted himself entirely and emphatically stated that indeed, this *was* her home and she should not *think* of moving and he would never *dream* of urging her to do something against her will. He brought his hand

[222]

down on his knee as if to close the deal. 'Well, Louisa, may I tell Margaret you'll be our guest on Christmas Day?'

'Thank you very much, Mr Shillingcote, but if my health permits I shall go to my cousin Enid's in Shepherd's Bush.'

'Your health, Louisa? Surely you haven't been —'

'Oh no, Mr Shillingcote. I'm quite fit, more fit than a woman my age has any right to expect. Now you wait here and let me go and fetch the tea and your bottle of Christmas Cordial.'

She vanished into the kitchen and left him there with his mental calculations, turning square feet into pounds and pence, all the while congratulating himself on his generosity of spirit in asking Louisa Wyatt to join them for Christmas, the feeling all the sweeter knowing she would decline. She had come once, in 1968, very early on in their acquaintance, and not since, but every year he asked her, as part of the Christmas spirit, offering this aged, friendless woman the considerable pleasures of his table, his wine cellar, his own stellar company and that of his wife, Margaret, who, after the 1968 débâcle had vowed to divorce him if he ever brought that thankless, potty, garrulous insufferable old hag home with him again. *And,* Margaret sniffed, *I don't care if the old girl owns an entire block of flats in Westminster Abbey!* Because on her 1968 Christmas visit, Louisa Wyatt had criticized the cooking at every turn, not in a nasty fashion, only as a disinterested cookery expert. Nothing was quite right, none of the flavors quite balanced, nor the skin on the goose quite as crackling as it ought to have been and the oysters hadn't that saltwater tang of the very best, the very freshest which was impossible to come by nowadays anyway because everyone knew all waters were polluted and —

Mrs Shillingcote, striving for polite equilibrium, had

inquired if Louisa did much cooking and the old woman had rolled her eyes and said never, adding that she was expert, just the same, from reading old cookbooks, and then Louisa had launched into a long disquisition, beginning with her chance discovery that day so very long ago at the Bodleian Library and culminating with her 1957 discovery of Lady Aylesbury's hand-transcribed cookbook in Ye Spinning Wheel which used to be Featherstone's Rare Books in Woodstock before the tourists got to it.

It was the wine. That's what Louisa was thinking in the kitchen as she gathered the tray and remembered that dreadful 1968 Christmas with the Shillingcotes. She'd drunk far too much wine. She was unaccustomed to drinking at all and somehow, in a dithery and inexplicable way, had confused the drinking of wine with the reading of drinking of wine, enjoying Margaret Shillingcote's wine as though it were Lady Aylesbury's, not realizing that one may read of drinking as much as one wishes with few ill effects, but to actually put it into practice in one's life . . . well. That was a wholly different matter. Rather like squandering love, she thought as she placed the bottle of Christmas Cordial on the tray and went back toward the sitting-room. One might read of squandered love with nothing more than a few pangs and sniffles, but to endure it . . .

She set the tray before Mr Shillingcote and he regarded the bottle of Christmas Cordial with the relish he might have donated to a perfectly-grilled chop. 'We are looking forward to our Christmas Cordial, Louisa,' he said with a wink. In fact since 1968 his wife had dumped each bottle of Christmas Cordial on the houseplants and though she had remarked to her husband that very morning at breakfast that the philodendron had grown a full foot and a half after last year's dousing, he thought it best not to submit this fact in evidence of its efficacy. 'Excellent stuff, your cordial.'

'"The vertues of this water"', Louisa began as she poured his tea and passed him a stale biscuit, '"are many. It provoketh urine and preventeth the gravel and the stone. It helpeth against the pantings and swimming of the braine. It cureth contractions of the sinews. It preserveth the heart against envy," Mr Shillingcote. "Whomsoever shall drink of this water shall be made content and to know the manifold pleasures of life."'

When Basil Shillingcote finally left, Louisa saw him to the front door, closed it after him and stayed there, just for a moment, bracing herself against its comfortable timbers. Mr Shillingcote had overstayed, she thought, walking slowly back to the sitting-room and hefting the tea tray. Seeing the tea still warm in his cup she wondered if her estimation were correct and was about to say something to Julian when he reminded her (in his husbandly way) that she had best turn off the electric fire before returning to the kitchen. 'Oh yes,' she said absently. 'A pity to waste all this warmth.' And though she would have liked to linger there with Julian, it was the night before Christmas Eve and she had work to do before she could go to bed: the bottles to be readied for the milkman, the postman, the two dustmen and Enid.

She carried the tray back to the kitchen and considered the possibilities for supper. Frozen fish fingers presented themselves, but the very thought made her queasy. A cup of tea. That's what she needed.

The cup of tea did not quite have the restorative effect she had counted on, but she busied herself with the bottles just the same, flipping through her ribbon box and mentally designating colors: two blues for the dustmen, a yellow for the postman, green for the milkman. The milkman's green-banded bottle (labeled with a small card wishing him season's greetings from Miss Wyatt) she took to the front door and left it on the porch for him to collect in his early-morning rounds. The bottles for the dustmen and the postman she would give them personally the next day. She took a bottle and put it on the shelf beside the sink, glancing at herself in the darkened window, her own familiar features somehow oddly awry.

She returned to the table, picking through the ribbon box, fancying a red ribbon for Enid's bottle and not finding any. She thought she remembered seeing red ribbon in the drawer of the dressing table of her sister's old room. Or was it in her mother's dressing-table? She would look. For the jaunt upstairs she bundled up, buttoning her cardigan and throwing the mothy scarf around her neck, and took with her the bottle to store.

Every year Louisa kept one bottle of the cordial by the kitchen sink in case she should need it for some momentary infirmity or failure of spirit. (And she had used it in 1968 to ward off the hangover resulting from the disaster at the Shillingcotes'.) And one bottle she stored in the wardrobe of her parents' bedroom, the wardrobe in which her mother's 1905 wedding dress still hung, as though there might yet be a bride to wear it. (Louisa's sister, befitting a wartime bride, had worn a trim tailored suit for her wedding to the Arizona Yank.) Her mother's wedding dress always seemed to Louisa to be appropriate company for the many bottles of Christmas Cordial that had accumulated over the years since she had first read Lady Aylesbury's gorgeous script and heard – in a manner of speaking – her cool cultivated voice telling of the "vertues of this water" and her precise and elaborate rendering of the twenty-five different herbes and spices to be laid in faire water and then dried, bruised, stamped and shredded, added to ye

[226]

best gascoyne wine and let steep before distilling in a limbeck with a gentle fire. As Louisa made her way laboriously up the stairs to her parents' room, she found she could not remember a single memorable thing about any of the Christmases she had so carefully stored and laid away; they all seemed to mull together silently, even sadly, the way one feels at the sight of ribbon and wreath frozen in a January gutter.

Of course, she told herself, as she flipped on the overhead light in her parents' front bedroom, everything might have been different if Julian had lived, even, she reasoned, if her brothers had lived, if they'd come home from the war, if they'd married and had families, if her sister had not married the Yank and emigrated, if there had been children and grandchildren and perhaps even a fat baby great-grandchild, if – *if*. 'Pull yourself together,' she commanded herself, 'before your humours get unbalanced and the melancholia –' Her breath came in short swift stabs, slicing between her ribs like a knife, her pulse raced, her head pounded, pounded and she gripped the pineapple-topped poster of her parents' bed, hugged and clung to it as though begging it to dance, as her feet slid out from underneath her and she tumbled sprawling senselessly to the floor.

Pull yourself together. She could not speak, but she could think, slowly, *I can think*, and in doing so she thought of the telephone a full flight down; she thought of tomorrow, the 24th, when no one would miss her at the Explorers' Club because no one worked that day; she thought how Enid would not miss her till Christmas Day; she thought how she might die and not be missed at all and how her stockings had holes in them and her underwear not the freshest and her skirt splotched and the hem pinned up and how she would die, splayed on the floor of

[227]

her parents' room like a tiny rag doll carelessly thrown down by a pouting child and how she'd not accounted for an heir to the house and how she would be the only ghost here when the wrecking ball came through and chucked her into the street. *Pull yourself together*, she wept before succumbing again to the darkness in her head.

The clock in her parents' room was of the winding variety and had not been wound in thirty years and so Louisa Wyatt hadn't any idea how long she'd lain there on the floor, except that when she next blinked she could see it was still dark out and the blaring overhead light burnt into her squinting eyes and hurt them. Slowly she issued a series of commands to her body, some of which it obeyed and some it did not. She was aghast to discover that her urine had been provoked and since her next thought was of her mother's blue rug, she assured herself she was not only not dead, but not about to die. *Not yet. Not now. Oh please not now not now now now no not.* Though why *not now* she could not say. Was it that she hadn't yet 'done something' with her life? Because it was Christmas?

Death heeds no holidays and seemed intent on prying Louisa Wyatt's bony fingers from what little life she had left, but she silently struck a bargain: if Death would allow her to get up on the bed, at least to be found like a lady, in bed, composed as a lady ought to be, then she would go quietly. (She had no intention whatever of keeping this bargain, but thought it prudent to make.)

With a monstrous effort of will and using only the right side of her body, since the left side had died already, Louisa dragged herself along the floor beside the bed; she noted that the bottle of Christmas Cordial lay directly in her path and as she was inching and heaving she considered the many vertues of this water and thought it a shame she hadn't the strength to pull

[228]

open the cork and take the proverbial swig against what ailed her, assailed her and would doubtlessly defeat her. *But not yet. Not just yet. Not just now.* She clutched the bottle in her right hand, just for comfort and considered the most efficient way to heave her bones from the floor up to the high, beckoning bed. She raised herself to a slumped sitting position, resting her back against the bed and it then occurred to her that she had teeth. Her own in fact. Most of them. She raised the bottle to the right side of her mouth and urged her lips to open, to bare her teeth, much as Molly had bared her gleaming orthodontic work. Louisa's teeth obeyed and she shoved the cork between those teeth and commanded them to close. Her teeth seemed to hold a conference to decide if they would obey or not. Reluctantly they clamped around the cork. Louisa realized she was confronted with a difficult choice, indeed, a gamble: she probably did not have the strength to yank this bottle open with her teeth *and* get up on the bed, to die like a lady, to rise to the occasion. If she opted for the bottle, she might well die sprawled on the floor like an insect. She considered the possibilities and like the heroine she had never been, took the gallant path, used her every morsel of strength to yank on the bottle while imploring her teeth to keep their grip on the cork. The fluid gurgled out over her sweater and down her collar and stained her mother's blue rug before she could get the bottle to stand upright in her hand. And spit out the cork.

Haltingly Louisa raised the bottle to the right side of her mouth (which she thought was still open) and the Christmas Cordial splashed over her chin and ran down her neck and washed over her lips and teeth and tongue, or as much as she could feel of her lips and teeth and tongue. She swallowed as best she could. Again and again, she prayed that the vertues of this water were such that it would give her the strength to cast her body up on the bed in which she'd been conceived and brought forth, a squalling infant, three quarters of a century ago.

Before she could quite focus, the overhead light pricking her eyes the way Lady Aylesbury advised pricking cracknells before putting them like mackroons in a pritty hot oven, Louisa was besieged by sounds of crashing buckets and tinkling harps, the playing of the merry organ's sweet singing in her ear along with the rustle of satin, a whiff of coriander, clove and orange, a spray of ye wilde time brushed under her nose while the glow of a million golden candles melted the frost that wept its crystalline way down down down into the bowels of the city to escape the bombs, to huddle with strangers, with thumping good-natured wenches and blustering boys, footmen and handmaidens, with Anne, Lady Aylesbury, her voice graceful and culti- vated as her handwriting, turning to a portly well-fed, wigged and waistcoated man beside her and asking if the cordial wasn't just a bit tart this year and he, taking a pinch of snuff and eyeing his marriageable daughter who was enjoying the attentions of an impecunious younger son, applies the snuff to his nose and begins in stentorian tones that the vertues of this water are such that he sneezes and Mr Turner, the American sitting there beside him completes his thought in saying jo- vially that whomsoever shall drink thereof shall be caused to look youthful, Mr Shotworth contributing that it comforteth the vital spirits and restoreth the humours to their proper balance, easeth the swimming of the braine and Mrs Jobson, refilling her glass yet again from the decanter of ye best gascoyne wine, laughs and adds it cureth the contractions of the sinews, the hangover and (Mrs Jobson rising unsteadily, lifts her glass with a rousing hurrah) *Goodbye PMS!* which nets her some cheers from the women while Aunt Charlotte, fingering a stalk of candied angelica, inquires discreetly of Aunt Jane what *is* PMS and Aunt Jane, giving a nudge to a quaking jelly of damson plums beautifully unmolded before her, remarks to Louisa's mother that living without a husband is difficult, but not impossible, calls on Aunt Tilda to corroborate, but Tilda is smitten unto speechlessness at the sight of Lady Aylesbury's gown, textured and compounded in the bittersweet hue of Seville orringes, a string of pomegranate seeds beaded with currants around her neck, gleaming like jewels in the candlelight, the reflected warmth of the charcoal braziers, while 24-carat Jordan almonds drip from her ears as Lady Aylesbury wordlessly instructs a bevy of eager servants, their cheeks made ruddy from the kitchen, to bring up steaming silver platters and lay them before the guests, to see to their comfort and joy, such that Diana Dufour turns to the famous Imperial Explorer Sir William Barry seated beside her, marveling that *this, clearly this* is the Family of Man as it was intended to be and both Sir William Barry and Sir Clive Rackham rattle their goblets as they have rattled the parquet and wainscoting in the Explorers Club, they rattle and nudge Sir Matthew Curtis (the slayer of Pip) and all four laugh heartily, reminding Diana that it is the Family of Man and thensome with a nod and knowing snort to Pip sitting beside Sir Matthew Curtis (who is cracking his knuckles and walnuts, the shells of the latter dropped without ceremony into his amber port) and Pip roars his agreement, the expression of outrage softened by years of acceptance and a wreath of holly strung rakishly over his polar bear brow, the wreath slipping as Pip roars with hearty laughter gusting the candlelight before them and the holly and the ivy threading down the long table to where the uncomprehending, certainly irritated and vaguely out-raged Shillingcotes sit beside the bewildered Enid, burping Jack and Molly, Margaret Shillingcote describ-ing in a shrill voice Louisa's disgraceful conduct that Christmas of 1968 for the edification of the slack-jawed Enid and the sneer of wonderment highlighting Molly's heavy-metal mouth till Lady Aylesbury's cool culti-vated voice interrupts Margaret and gently but firmly reminds them that it is all very well to read of these things, drinking wine and squandering love, but to do them is quite another fa la la la la altogether just before she directs her beneficent attention to the flatulent Jack and inquires after his wambling belly, asks if he hasn't found the vertues of this water to be such that it cureth the griping belly, the lethargie, the frensie and madness of the war in Angola Colonel Stanhope is saying to a lady who sniffs a pomander ball in a manner at once coy and suggestive, offering the old soldier a muskadine comfit which causes the admiring Mr Taft, sitting near by, to rise to his feet and raise a toast to luck with the ladies and luck with horses, a proposal drunk with much gusto by everyone save for the displaced priests, upset and uprooted by the dissolution of the monasteries, on whom Lady Aylesbury lavishes, extolls her most calm-ing grace, her skin the color of a honey of roses, her gown spun from sparkling loaf sugar, a necklace of candied violets ringing her neck and tiny brittle mint cakes gleaming on her fingers, she smiles and says, God rest ye merry, gentlemen and ladies, it came upon a midnight clearly we've not yet come to our guest of honor, she adds, rising, the whiff of her compounded court perfume combining with the smoke spiraling from a million candles and the steam off a capon roste with oysters and a peacock roasted and draped again in its own finery set fragrantly before Louisa's proud father (claret glowing ruby in his appreciative hand) and Louisa's still lovely, always right and upright mother, her brothers in their unstained uniforms who sit beside the dustmen in their blue uniforms and the milkman in his and the postman (his fraying ring of hair covered by his cap) in his, all of them smiling and stuffing marchpane cakes into their cheeks and pockets as they laugh to the tune of the music wafting over them and wax on about the vertues of this water while Lady Aylesbury addresses them all, priests and polar bear alike, to tell them of all the things Louisa Wyatt hath done with her life, of those she helpeth and preserveth, of those she comforteth and restored, of all the time zones she has passed through and at this, Mr Shotworth (seated nearby Mr Featherstone and an eighteenth-century dowager with bosoms like two enormous boiled puddings), drops the bones of roasted plover upon which he has been nibbling and leaps to his feet, glass in hand, to announce that Louisa Wyatt, in recognition of her explorations into the past, is hereby granted Honorary Membership with All Privileges Appertaining Thereunto in the Explorers' Club and a great cheer goes up and people say: *Here Here!* And some say *There There*, as one would to a pouting child, to golden-haired moppets, a bouncing girl in a dress of jolly holly green sitting beside a small boy with his father's dark eyes, long lashes and small mouth, restless and listening as best they can as the guests exuberate upon the vertues of this water and their mother, their mother who loved the beautiful young people they would become when they went up to Oxford and embarked on lives (Lady Aylesbury was saying) of reckless virtue; *In Louisa Wyatt, I give you a life of reckless virtue, of gallant service, of unstinting imaginative energy, rendered lovingly, gen-erously and cordially* (the guests all laugh) *to those who were closest to her, and those who were not* (a chilly glance bestowed on Margaret Shillingcote), *to the living and the dead. Louisa Wyatt, who did not make those vulgar distinctions between what might have been and what was, a woman who, in this joyous season, offereth comfort and joy to all,* continues Anne, Lady Aylesbury whose dress has turned golden and light as puff pastry, the billowing sleeves elaborately beaded with caraway and anise seed, with bilberries and gooseberries, the bodice escalloped in perfectly sliced peaches preserved from some long-past summer, flounced with caramel ribbons in the style of a long time ago when she turns to Julian and smiles at him, sitting as he rises. And as he does, the music slowly stills, the last notes gleaming at the edge of hushing voices because Julian gives them all his wonderful grin, impertinent and cheerful, and he addresses them with a flash of David Niven and a dash of Leslie Howard and says to the assembled company that *we are come here today to celebrate what Louisa Wyatt has done with her life, to celebrate Louisa Wyatt, who, with equal parts joy and love has protected us all, the living and the dead, against the brutal hand of Time which would have seen us cast into the heap of the unremembered, Louisa Wyatt, who, with the most skill-ful of hands, each year unites that delicate elixir of memory and imagination and twenty-five different herbs and spices, laide in faire water bruised, shredded, dried and combined with the best gascoyne wine, steep-ed over days and then distilled on a gentle fire to be brought forth every Christmas season in a cordial, the vertues of which are manifold, a water to dispell the soot and grime of compromise, my friends, the accretion of smoke from dreams long snuffed out, the exhaust of*

*idling lives, the dust of fear and hope denied, oh my dear
Louisa* – Julian turns to her, his too-small mouth poised
in its beautiful, familiar smile – *oh Louisa, I love you so*

'It's so! I tell you she ain't missed a Christmas in fifteen
years and the bloke before me said she 'adn't missed a
Christmas with him neither, so I'm telling your bleeding bobby lordship, there's something wrong and you
got to go in there!'

'And I tell you, I can't. Not without a warrant.'

'Bugger the warrant! She's old. She must be ninety!
She gives me a bottle of this stuff every December 24th
and she ain't there today and *it* ain't there today and
something terrible's gone on.' The postman mopped his
face against the choler and unexpected anger.

The police sergeant behind the desk regarded the
postman indulgently. 'She might have gone away for
the holidays. Think of that, did you? Lots of people
leave on Christmas Eve.'

'Not Miss Wyatt.'

'Fancy yourself a friend of the family, do you?'

'Look, she ain't got any family. She's a hundred years
old, see? She's got no one and she's all alone in that big
house and while you're clacking your jaws, she might be
on the edge of life and death, she might be drawing her
last while the London police diddles their doorknobs
over warrants and –'

'The law's the law.'

'Oh, that's a good one. Tell me about the law. You'd
see it different if she was some punk in the Tube station
shot full of –'

'That's enough,' the sergeant announced, heaving his
bones out of the chair and adding that he would be right
back. The postman took off his cap and ruffled his
fraying ring of hair, his fraying patience which was tried

[235]

to the last when the sergeant returned and said the London police could do nothing about an old woman who always left a bottle with a ribbon on it on the porch for the postman every December 24, advising the postman to get back to his rounds if he knew what was good for – but just then the two dustmen burst into the station and hurried to the desk and said their bottles (ribbons and all) had not been left in the alley for them and at that the sergeant threw up his hands and called the hospital and eventually an ambulance wailed through the streets of London, braying its way towards Holland Park, to the only house not cut up into flats where they found the postman and the two dustmen awaiting them on the steps. The police came too because a crowd gathered and it was necessary to contain them so that a half-dozen men could force the door of the woman known only to them as Miss Wyatt. Amidst the haste and commotion, the confusion and excitement, no one noticed that in the windows fronting the street, all the frost that usually ringed them had melted, as though the heat and hope and human expiration of a great many people had combined to warm those otherwise empty rooms.

THE FOOT

Helen Harris

When I found the foot, I felt very happy. I had been wandering all day, for days, through the streets of the city and I was acutely conscious of my feet. They had carried me mutely, like donkeys, up and down the hills of the city, powerless to do otherwise, and here was a foot with autonomy. I sat down in the shadow of the cloister which lined the courtyard, where the sun was glittering on the mosaics and the goldfish pond, and I spread my dusty toes and grinned.

Giselle had driven me away from England. At the time, I had been bitter and resentful; setting out on my travels on the cross-Channel ferry on an overcast day, sitting in the steamed-up bar and looking out at the unpleasant grey sea. My bad temper travelled with me through France, the spring, cold still and a pale wet grey, too early for anyone to set out on a journey like this of their own accord. I watched myself, a sorry figure I thought, a brown-haired athletic young man in his late thirties, sitting alone night after night in restaurants and in bars, and walking, endlessly walking himself into a state of exhaustion because a young woman who was incapable of recognizing her own happiness had sent him away.

In the Val d'Aosta, I think my gloom began to lift. It was such a desolate place that northern spring, where working men with respiratory diseases coughed and coughed and bolstered themselves with leaden pasta against the cold seeping out of the mountains. In contrast, my own life seemed so light just then. I could move on in the morning and leave behind the chest complaints and the overhanging mountains, which I did, always moving south, into Yugoslavia and then Greece. As I travelled, and the lukewarm spring grew into a full-blown southern summer, my bad temper became more and more of a pose and less and less a real feeling, until one morning on Rhodes, I caught myself walking down a street in the sunshine with a spontaneous smile on my face. It struck me then how foolish it was to stamp my way south, as I had been, with my face set in a determined frown, like a punished schoolboy in knee-socks. The character of my journey changed; instead of a sullen, self-pitying flight from a woman who had rejected me, it turned into the extended wanderings of a sensible single man.

So Giselle had rejected me. But was that a reason to ruin the rest of my life? When I thought about her, which I did every night in the bedrooms of a succession of cheap hotels, watching car headlights slide across the warty ceilings, it was easy to remember her faults, all the qualities which my ideal woman would come without. I cured myself that way of a good deal of my bitterness. And, during the day, I took a vindictive pleasure in ogling the Greek women in a way I would never have dreamt of doing in England, just to spite her memory. On Rhodes, strolling out alone into the golden morning, I started to enjoy my journey. Only at the back of my mind, there still hung a shadow, as out of place in the Mediterranean summer as a raincoat left hanging in a cupboard.

Giselle was the daughter of a famous composer. It would not have been more classical nor more ridiculous if he had been a philosopher or a poet. He was very famous, very gifted, very respected, and Giselle worshipped him. She and her father lived together in a large rather dark flat, full of imposingly valuable possessions: the lamps were antique, if you accidentally broke a piece of china, it would be a tragedy. The flat had double doors between its series of interconnecting rooms. They were always either open on one side or ajar a specific amount or intentionally shut and the position of the doors dominated the flat. You had to notice their position when you entered a room so you could carefully repeat it when you left. This wasn't neurosis, Giselle insisted, when I made fun of it; it was to avoid draughts, light falling on valuable paintings, and above all noise, noise penetrating to her father's study. The doors were never both wide open.

Her mother had died when she was a child and her father had not remarried. He and Giselle lived in a tight, mutually totally satisfying relationship, which it would have been impossible for a second wife to enter. Indeed, this was very largely the reason why my own bid for Giselle failed. The two of them essentially preferred each other to everyone else.

Giselle did not remember very much about her mother. I think, in her subconscious, she considered her irrelevant, a necessary but otherwise unimportant part of the process of creating her perfect bond with her father. She assumed that theirs had been a story-book happy marriage because anything else could have been a criticism of her father. But the truth was she had no idea; when I questioned her about it once, in the build-up to an argument, it became clear that she knew nothing about it, to the extent that she did not even know how many years before her birth her parents had married. She pointed once, in evidence, to the fact that her father had never remarried. But it was pretty plain to anyone who knew Richard that this could equally well have been due to cautious self-protecting retirement from ups and downs and disturbances, or as it seemed to me, because he had all he needed in Giselle.

I met Giselle at the theatre. My friend Rowena Blake had organized one of those exquisitely awkward evenings in which she specialized, where half a dozen people who had never met, with maybe nothing in common beyond their acquaintance with Rowena, were introduced in the foyer, sat down in a row to watch the play and then held a stilted conversation over drinks afterwards. How ludicrous it all seems, viewed from this shirt-sleeved climate. I was seated next to Giselle. It was a terribly close July evening in London; I dare say the last thing any of us wanted to do was to go to the theatre. What I first noticed about Giselle was how formally she was dressed, despite the stuffy evening. All the other girls were bare-legged, in sandals, but Giselle was wearing fine mesh tights and high-heeled navy and white court shoes. Her dress had a large navy and white bow under the chin.

But she was not 'old maidish'. In fact, when I turned to her and said, 'I'm Edward Thorne. I'm sorry, I missed your name', I was struck by the light in her face, a light which you usually only see in the faces of very attractive women who know they continue to captivate their husband or lover. Now Giselle, much as I love, loved her, was only ever elegant; she was not a beauty. I was so struck by her light because it did not appear to have any source in what I quickly found out about her life; she was unmarried and unattached at thirty, a fate which I always supposed women dreaded, and she was living what sounded a glum life with her widowed father, working, not because she needed to, as secretary to a paediatric surgeon. Her confidence intrigued me.

I said, 'What else have you seen by Stoppard?' and she answered poisedly, '*Rosencrantz and Guildenstern Are Dead* and *Every Good Boy Deserves Favour.*'

That was typical of Giselle; she never asked you to buy cherry jam but Maraschino cherry jam, she never read *Brideshead* but '*Brideshead Revisited* by Evelyn Waugh'.

She was an impeccable secretary. The paediatric surgeon, an old-school surgeon with works of art in his consulting rooms, so appreciated having her there, in her lovely outfits, with her calm gentle manners, that he paid her astronomical wages, which she never needed. He was, I believe, an extremely capable surgeon. He had perfected an operation to remedy a congenital heart defect in children and he particularly appreciated the delicate way Giselle dealt with his youngest patients. I developed a dream of turning Giselle from an impeccable secretary into an impeccable wife and giving her children of her own to care for.

When I think of courting Giselle, which took one summer and one winter, I think of her striking appearances. I lived for them; I waited for them in her sitting-room, at exhibitions and in restaurants, wherever we had agreed to meet. She always came up to my expectations; stepping poisedly through doorways, round corners, with her head held high and an expression of serene self-possession on her marmoreal face. She always had a hat, a hair-do, a handbag, which lifted her outfit from mere elegance to something quite stunning. I think of the sound of her high heels tapping beside me, tapping deliciously, impaling my emotions on their swaying spikes.

At last, she condescended to me and we entered the strange guarded incomplete relationship which was to last until this spring. Giselle allowed me to approach her but I was left in the morning, not feeling that I had claimed her but that she had temporarily been kind enough to let me visit. The circumstances in which this took place seem very significant, with hindsight.

Her father was in Munich at a festival. A new work of his was to be performed in public for the first time. Giselle would normally have gone with him but the surgeon was scheduled to carry out a number of major operations and he had specifically asked Giselle not to take any holiday at this important time. But the real reason was that her father's agent, a capable, well-groomed, middle-aged woman whom she did not like called Barbara Sims, was going with him and Giselle was not needed.

She cooked me dinner in the empty flat. This was already a marked change from our formal evenings of theatres, taxis, restaurants, helping Giselle on with her coat, blowing her kisses as she closed her front door. It was April and it was raining. She made watercress soup, trout with almonds and lemon mousse. We ate ceremonially in the silent flat.

It always seemed to me incongruous that someone as slender, as thin as Giselle should cook with such care and affection; her long thin hands bearing dishes of rich meat in thick alcoholic sauces to the table. It is only now that I see she used food to reinforce the distinction between herself, ethereal, infinitely refined and delicate, and everyone else, a slave to their crude material appetites.

After the meal, we had coffee and cognacs beside each other on the settee. Giselle had kicked one of her feet free of her narrow shiny black shoes and it dangled next to me, long, white and arching, her slim toes curling and uncurling as they savoured their new found freedom. I bent and stroked it and Giselle laughed, a clear, high-pitched laugh which contained pleasure and surprised amusement and condescension. Encouraged, I slipped off the settee and, kneeling in front of her, I took her foot tenderly in my hands and began to kiss it. High above me, I heard her still laughing, a distant, entertained laugh, so far away it seemed incorporeal, quite unattached to the long white foot.

In the morning, our life together began, in her childhood bedroom, behind its pastel-flowered curtains. For a week of her father's absence, we led a charmed life in that bedroom, making love sedately each morning and each evening, as though it were a grave formal dance, and Giselle setting out my breakfast for me on the dark dining-room table.

The night before her father returned, Giselle said to me that of course we couldn't continue the same way any more once he came back. If I wanted to 'visit' her, as she put it, I must come during the day; I couldn't sleep the night there once her father was back. I was extremely put out. I didn't expect, at the age of thirty-six, to be confronted with parental obstacles once more. I had a small house of my own in a suburb. Giselle had, for some reason or other, never seen it. I said to her, why couldn't she come and spend the night there if she was concerned about offending her father? She compressed her lips and she shook her head firmly. She didn't even offer me an explanation; she simply wasn't prepared to let her father find out that she had a lover.

'Tell him you're staying with a girl-friend', I said, annoyed with myself, even as I said it, for slipping so easily back into teenage subterfuges. Giselle looked, rightly, disgusted and she didn't answer me.

I had to 'visit' her secretively during the day, when we were neither of us working or if I came in the evening, I had to be heard to leave before midnight. Our lovemaking, always cautious and delicate, became as fragile as bone china.

[245]

That stage lasted for three months. In July, her father went to his summer retreat in the South of France. In the normal course of events, Giselle would have gone with him but, for some reason, instead she stayed with me. By then, I have to admit, I was completely obsessed with her. Otherwise, I do not think I would have put up with all she submitted me to. But I was infatuated with her; I was even infatuated with her footprints in talcum powder on the bathroom floor. I didn't wipe them away so I could still look at them when she was gone. I must have been quite blinkered not to realize that it would have been far more pleasant and more natural for both of us to join her father in France.

He stayed in St Paul de Vence until the first of September. I think those two months were the best time Giselle and I ever had. Certainly, looking back at them now from this dry bare landscape, I can only remember verdant happy scenes, only joy.

Giselle came to stay at my house, which was at once transformed into a beautiful haven. I think of her hands arranging flowers in vases in my sitting-room. That summer, for the first time, I asked her to marry me. She laughed, a clear high-pitched laugh which contained surprised amusement and condescension. She shook her head and she twitched, as though a fly had landed on her. I grabbed her by the wrist – we were lying in bed together – and I exclaimed, 'Why not? Can't you see that's the only solution?' But she just laughed and shook her head and said, 'Don't say things like that, Edward.' She tried to make up for the hurt of her rejection by doing something tender which she knew I liked; placing the cool sole of her foot on the small of my back and pressing.

It is impossible to determine the moment when the rot set in, when things began to come apart. If you

believe that the end is contained in seed in the beginning, then things began to come apart the evening I first
kissed Giselle's feet.

'You are married to your father,' I told her, 'you know
it's high time you grew up and left him.'

'You're the one who should grow up,' she answered
petulantly, 'you should learn to stand on your own two
feet.'

But when she refused to stay with me, I was desolate.
Once or twice, even during those two months, she had
to stay the night at her father's; to receive his pre-
arranged telephone calls, to let in his cleaning lady in
the morning. There was no arguing with these con-
cessions to her father's convenience. If I protested, I only
ran the risk that she would simply stay away longer.

Between her father's return and Christmas, we spent
at most six nights together, when her father was away
lecturing, or abroad. I had begun bitterly to resent
Richard's shadow, hanging like a stern guardian over
us; a possessive husband, who had no right to possess
her. At some point, I think when Richard was ill with
influenza and she stayed away from me all week to nurse
him, it occurred to me to question whether this bond
was equally mutual; did her father depend on her as
intensely as she depended on him? I imagined a very
base all male conspiracy; if he didn't, if the obsession
was even slightly lopsided, then I could maybe fall in
league with him and by becoming his friend, persuade
him that I was an ideal partner for his daughter.

Richard had by now noticed that I was something
more than a casual acquaintance of Giselle's, although
how much he had worked out from his seclusion, I
wasn't certain. He didn't seem to dislike me and, starting by expressing an intelligent interest in his music, I
began to court him.

Giselle and Richard watched me. Giselle was pleased, I think, in spite of herself, that I had begun to show a liking for her father. But she was wary, oh, we both were, of each other's every move; stepping round each other on tiptoe in a diminishing circle. Richard simply couldn't be bothered; he knew I was there and he spoke to me, but there was a place where his attention ended. Inside that place, he lived quite content with his music.

At mealtimes, on the rare occasions when we all three ate together, I did my desperate best to seduce them. I was charming, entertaining, miserable. I told tragically funny stories, I made fun of myself, and Richard at the head of the table and Giselle opposite me listened to me with similarly condescending expressions on their similar faces. Richard once questioned me, a little dubiously, about my work; clearly he couldn't quite envisage what someone as pedestrian as a solicitor actually did. But, in my desperation, I interpreted even this question as a positive sign; he was considering my stability, my worth as a wage-earner. I was like a puppy, I realized, cavorting for scraps at their dinner table.

The dog-like character of my devotion hit me in the end, as it had to, and negated the year of happiness, the images I still cherish absent-mindedly of Giselle in my dreams: the open doors of her dark heavy wardrobe, inside which her pale clothes are like butterflies pinned in a lepidopterist's case, and her shoes and boots and sandals lined up in the bottom in rows, while in front of the wardrobe, playing with one gilt handle, Giselle stands in her stocking feet and asks me teasingly, 'Which is it to be then, Edward, the mules or the thongs?' Giselle's polka-dot summer sundress, which she always wore with a pair of teetering white multiply-strapped sandals; the dress and a hat and the sandals laid out ready in her bedroom while she takes a bath in the adjoining bathroom. I am sitting on the bed, waiting, and through the open bathroom door I am watching Giselle, who has lifted one long leg up in the air and is soaping herself delicately between the toes.

We spent a laughable sort of Christmas. I was invited to lunch on Christmas Day, along with two infirm aunts and other sorry relatives. I helped Giselle fetch and carry from the kitchen and I chauffeured the aunts home when the afternoon was over. I came back to find Giselle and Richard sipping port in their armchairs in the sitting-room, comfortably ensconced like an elderly couple, who made a sterling effort at sociability to greet me.

'Ah, pull up a chair,' said Richard kindly, 'we were just saying we reckoned you'd earned a breather.'

But before sitting down, I dutifully topped up his port, on a nod from Giselle.

Yes, I see myself in that period as a lap-dog. I sat with them unhappily all evening, resentfully listening to Richard reminisce, and at night, ever though I literally ached to possess Giselle, I had to go home unrequited because on Christmas Day there was no hope that she would desert Richard.

Things were not right by then even on the rare occasions when we could spend a night together. My frenzy made me ungraceful and I did not want to sleep at all so I could keep a hold on Giselle. Repeatedly she complained that I woke her because even in my sleep I huddled so hard against her, clinging, quivering, breathing my unwelcome canine breath on her and, once, humiliatingly, I woke her with my extraordinary position, curled up at her feet, yes, just like a lap-dog.

I think it is not surprising, considering the lengths of frustration to which she drove me, that things should have come to an end the way they did. I was maybe guilty of excessive subservience, but Giselle was guilty of a stony indifference.

It was February and we were at a concert, Giselle and Richard and I. Once, as I say, I had been glad that we began to go out as a threesome, but I was long since sick of it. At that concert, as we sat prominently in the front row and people looked at Giselle and Richard, she reached for me and held my hand. For a moment, I was delighted. I held it fast and longed to turn and kiss her. The constraints of the concert limited me to a sneaking sideways look and her blank face baffled me. I gave her hand a conspiratorial squeeze but she did not squeeze back. Then I understood my purpose: I was there to prove to the world that there was nothing untoward between her and Richard. I was a handy young man they had brought out to dispel rumours. There, in front of the assembled music world, Giselle would fondle me, to show them Richard had nothing but a fatherly relationship with his daughter, and to preserve Richard's reputation.

For days after the concert, I did not ring her, plunged in the deepest of February gloom. At last, to my satisfaction, Giselle rang me. Her first words chilled me, unsatiated desire and all. 'Wherever have you been, Edward? We were getting quite worried.'

I answered nastily, 'Why? Does your father need another alibi?'

At Giselle's end, there was a shocked silence. Then she laughed, a clear high-pitched laugh of condescension. She said, 'Goodness, Edward, I don't know what you imagine.'

We had it out. I went over hot foot to their flat and we had it out in malicious whispers in Giselle's bedroom. She would neither confirm nor deny it. She only wrung her hands and crossed and uncrossed her legs and once she giggled. She said that was just the way I saw it.

Then, for several weeks, I did not speak to her, although in an underhand way I kept track of her movements. I watched the surgeon's door every day at the time she left his office. I rang their telephone late at night and until she hung up, I listened for voices. I was still obsessed even though I never spoke to her. And then in April, after nearly a month's silence, she sent me an invitation to an official dinner; her father was to receive another honorary doctorate and the pleasure of my company was requested. It was then I first thought of leaving the country because I understood that I was nothing more than a pedestal for Giselle to stand on.

That is why, when I found the foot, I felt so profoundly happy. It stood so sturdily alone. It had no need of a body. I squatted down beside it in the museum courtyard and tenderly examined its big marble mass. 'Foot of colossal sculpture. Ashkelon. Roman period,' read the accompanying caption. Down its grey length ran the criss-cross of Roman sandals. I followed it with my finger. Caressingly, I appreciated the nail on each fine toe.

I sat for a long time in the courtyard and the foot, which had at first sight seemed self-explanatory, started to raise all sorts of questions. For instance, what had happened to the body? There was no indication of any other stone limbs in the vicinity. The foot had been found alone. The jagged break of the stone at the ankle suggested destruction. But who would have carried off the pieces and left such a magnificent foot behind? No, I imagined some sort of voluntary severance. I don't know how, but I imagined the foot bounding off with giant hops through history. It had set out, free of its cumbersome colossal stone body and, after a long and enigmatic journey, had finally come to rest in this sunlit courtyard, to flex its giant toes for posterity beside the goldfish pond.

I thought about it later, as I walked back to my hostel in the old city, and in bed that night I remembered it. It would be supreme now, in the darkness, lording it over the silent courtyard, an enduring stone monument to independence.

As I travel further south, the landscapes growing drier and barer, and still I haven't met anyone whom I like even half as much as Giselle, I derive some satisfaction from the thought that the foot is there, shining in the moonlight.

A WELL-SPENT LIFE

Robert Edric

1

She had started holding séances during the war to capitalise on all the dead soldiers, distantly and uncertainly killed. Originally she'd charged five shillings a head, and then, moving in accord with the market demand, seven and ten; a pound for the wife of a Captain or above. The widows of the higher ranks tended to keep their grief and inquisitive urges to themselves, and there were fewer of them anyway; her real profit lay in the ranks. Her earnings rose and fell. She kept charts, and plotted the larger campaigns on maps she'd had since she was a girl.

She made her first small tax-free fortune during the BEF's half-hearted wanderings in Belgium and France; her second from the Western Desert, and then exceeded all her expectations with the Burma campaign and the Forgotten Army fighting it. The more distant the better: messages from the spirit world, she said, were like wine and travelled badly. Her little joke.

She had expected to reap the results of the D-Day landings, but by then a new and unwelcome wave of optimism was sweeping the country, a quickening of pace. At the time, someone had even suggested to her that what she was doing might be treasonous. The accusation worried her, but the demand persisted and there was still money to be made.

Forty comfortable years later she could still laugh. Comfortable by her own standards and her mother's standards; not comfortable by the standards of the women who went on stage to do what she did, or who wrote books, or appeared on television chat shows, but still comfortable. (She'd registered herself as self-employed in 1949.)

Even then, the majority of her clients had been mothers, wives and sweethearts still anxious to learn the truth about their sons, husbands, fiancés and lovers. And she told them precisely what they wanted to hear, and sympathised with them, and reassured them, and pointed the way ahead. Wasn't she a wife and mother herself? Hadn't she loved? They thanked her and said God bless her.

Well, no, in truth, she wasn't and hadn't.

Yes, yes, I see it all – pause, creased brow, pained expression, relax – Your husband died leading his men. I see a hill, your husband against the sky-line with his pistol drawn; I see him waving his men on and shouting encouragement to them. I see him – fade, smile, gone.

– Oh, you don't know how much it means to me to know that. Oh, I'm so grateful. Yes, I can see him; that was the kind of man he was.

(It was the kind of man they all were from 1942 onwards. A mental calculation sensibly upgrading the charge from five to seven shillings.)

Yes, he might only have been an engineer – only! – but there he is, holding off the enemy while his mates get to safety across the bridge (important word, 'mates') and then destroying it and himself with it. Oh, what a man, an unsung hero. (Important word, 'oh', for both parties.)

– That's him, the brave stupid fool. You don't know how much –

(Seven to ten shillings.)

'Brave stupid fool' were newspaper and cheap novel words.

And through it all she lived alone and with herself.

[256]

She developed civilian casualties as a sideline. The Blitz, bombings, V1s, V2s, shelling from offshore, torpedoed merchant seamen. Much of what she saw she'd already seen in films and newsreels: the officer leading his men with his pistol drawn, connected by a braided leather cord to his wrist, belonged to a different war entirely.

She asked to hold the telegrams and to be shown a photograph of the dead man; it was as much as she ever needed. Any mistakes and she could blame the Ministry (another useful word) or, as a last resort, the spirit world itself.

Her reputation spread. People, still mostly women, visited her in lieu of the funeral many of them had anticipated, but which few actually got.

And then the war ended.

There followed two lean years as she suffered and rode the new wave of rebuilding and looking ahead and the shunning of death. And then business gradually picked up again. She considered and then attempted building up a stage act, but she could not project herself sufficiently and the time was still not right.

She considered writing a book of her experiences – *Encouragement and spiritual help to those who still felt the need*. The publisher had written back asking to see her manuscript. Ah, well, with regard to that, she was afraid – No book. She did once, in 1956, sit down and try to write, but every sentence was knocked off balance with its three lies to every one truth, and even the truths were constituted of lies in the first instance. 'Perhaps with the advantage of hindsight –' the tenth publisher had suggested. She wrote to her regular clients asking for testimonials; few responded; most tried to talk her out of it; several absolved themselves completely from the flimsy web of self-deception.

[257]

She moved from London to Brighton and then back to London. She lost money on the sale of her property. She called herself by a new name, advertised, worked, dropped her prices before raising them, survived and then succeeded again.

In forty years she had put on a great deal of weight and was now frequently ill. When people commented on her being constantly out of breath she told them it was the price she had to pay, the cross she had to bear, the burden she . . . Someone from the spirit world had kept her awake all night, had demanded to possess her and had worn her out, exhausted her, depleted her. She forgave them all. She said the spirits were her children, childlike and restless, wandering and wanting only to be found. Just waiting to be contacted and put at ease. (But only by the people who were paying for and committed to her services, and who dare not dispute her for fear of disappointing only themselves.) Yes, of course, they replied, pulled out chairs for her, soothed her, made her tea, told her not to go on, to rest, that they could wait. But no, she had a duty to fulfil; she couldn't disappoint them.

She had a mission. Her burden had its compensations. Death held no fear for her. She had over £20,000 pounds in her building-society account and a similar sum invested elsewhere. When nothing else appeared to her during her sessions she imagined a house in Capri. Gracie Fields lived in Capri. She imagined Gracie Fields had once appeared to her and convinced her that Capri was exactly the place for a woman of her temperament, talents and deep understanding.

But to the truth . . . never once, in forty years, had she established any real contact, never once had she felt the rush of something – spirit or otherwise – entering her body, speaking through her and possessing her.

And now, being out of breath most of the time, even her 'voices' were difficult to produce. She sweated easily, and that, temporarily, helped appearances. There was nothing the doctors could do for her, nothing they could now tell her which she didn't already know. She'd been contacted by some of the finest minds of the past centuries. Ah, yes, they said, scarcely looking up from writing their prescriptions, the finest minds. She left their surgeries convinced she was right and they were wrong. She knew all there was to know about so many lies – or the same lie told so many times – making a truth. But did they?

She convinced herself that she'd come a long way in forty years. The more evidence *they* produced to dispute the existence of a spirit world, the more people needed *her* to tell them otherwise. She knew from recurrent visits how successful she was. She laughed easily at any mention of the word 'fraud'. She continued to tell her customers that their own receptivity was as necessary as her own gift for anything to be achieved; it made them feel involved. And, having paid their money –

In Brighton, she'd been visited by a succession of celebrities and entertainers there for the summer, all of whom had been photographed with her. But that had been Brighton, and they had been what they were. These days, thirty years on, people preferred to come and go without being noticed.

2

There was a narrow path through the long garden to her front door, and at the gate opening onto the street were two heavy lavender bushes which overhung and interlocked. The path was flanked by more lavenders, rhododendrons and laburnum bushes, the overall effect of which was best viewed from one of the upstairs rooms, where only she went, and then only rarely; she climbed the stairs only when she needed to.

The immediate effect upon entering the garden from the street was one of enclosure. The scent, when the flowers were in bloom, was overpowering, and clung to people in the house, which suffered as a result of the shade into which that part of it was perpetually cast.

She regretted the loss of the word 'sweetheart' because of its applicability to every situation and the manner (never offensive) in which it allowed mistakes to be made.

Her powers of recall and concentration were not what they had once been. Forty years, she said, was a long time to be frequently and often unexpectedly possessed by the spirits of great and active men. Women of the same age around the table secretly envied her. What men? When, where, how? Strictest confidence, she told them. They understood. They made bookings for repeat performances. They believed. The more vague and distant she became, the more allowances they were prepared to make for her.

All had gone well until her health had begun to deteriorate more rapidly. Other practitioners rose and continued rising around her. She denounced them as frauds and charlatans. A vogue developed for larger meetings and public spectacles with which she was unable to compete. But she survived.

Only in the past year had things started going really badly for her.

Notice had been given of a compulsory purchase order on the street in which she lived. Nothing urgent, but there all the same, a dark cloud hanging over the future, like the suggestion of her own death.

Someone from the local planning office had written to

tell her that the lavender bushes overhanging the street constituted a nuisance and that they had grown too large. Steps would have to be taken. Pruning? she'd written back. Felling, the council replied.

And now, to crown it all, a new church – a new *Catholic* church – was to be built on the site of the church directly opposite her home which had been destroyed by fire in 1973 and the rubble razed and cleared two years later. She had benefited from the existence of the consecrated, if derelict ground, had pointed it out, had suggested that it might be one of the sources of her – People listened, people believed. They were invited to the lace-curtained windows to peer out at it through the corridor of the lavenders, rhododendrons and laburnums.

She did not know what the construction of a new church would do to her trade. She'd seen the plans for the reconstruction of the whole area in the Town Hall. It was to be a big, spectacular church, and its longest shadow might even touch her home.

She'd gone to complain about the decision to fell the lavenders and saw immediately into what deeper and more treacherous waters she had fallen. Since then she'd stayed away and had left their letters unanswered. Every avenue of speculation led her to the same unhappy conclusion.

When business was bad – and it fell off quickly with the new development and the relocation of her regulars – she watched daytime television and continued to overeat.

A local Residents Association tried to solicit her support, but what could she do? What useful skills did she possess which they might – unless, of course, they considered her something of a local celebrity – No, they explained, her signature would have been enough.

The men with their axes held off coming.

During the winter the house became damper than usual. Repairs she should have had carried out ten years ago were now no longer necessary.

She held unattended séances and spoke to herself, telling anyone who might be listening of her troubles.

When her trade reached its lowest she was forced to wait until sufficient individuals had expressed an interest before arranging a séance to accommodate them all. More women worked during the day, and as a result she was forced into holding her sessions during the evenings. Before she began, the women sat around the table and complained of their aching feet or the price of food, or their husbands, or of the thousand other disappointments their lives held. She understood for the first time the true nature of the reasons for their visits.

Her séances catered to all tastes, something for every occasion. She held their hands and they linked up around the table. She'd already made her calculations: the most eager and susceptible of the group would be visited first, and her belief would become infectious. The sceptics would be disappointed simply because that was what they were. They would spoil it for the others, she suggested, and then displayed her charity and sympathy for them.

A new supermarket was built, a new clinic, a new community centre, a new play area. She visited them all and looked at them from the opposite side of the road. There were days when stepping from the road up onto the kerb left her breathless and gasping.

And then work on the new church began in earnest. The noise of the machinery and the shouts of the labourers filled her home. There was an urgency in everything the men did, and the shell of the church was due to be completed by late the following spring, early summer.

[262]

She watched them throw bricks to each other, catch them and lay them, and noted their progress from day to day. It was still winter, and the full extent of the shadow of the church was difficult to calculate.

She had never previously been aware of a Catholic population large enough to sustain such a project. (The destruction of the old church had always seemed to her to be the final act of something which had already run its natural course.)

There were days, and then weeks, when she became ill, and was unable to continue. She guessed she was dying, but how was she supposed to respond? Appearances and beliefs would, out of necessity, have to be maintained right up to the very end. And afterwards, because of what she'd spent a lifetime telling them, her customers would convince each other that she'd gone to a happier place, that she was among friends, that her physical restrictions and disabilities no longer mattered. At her few remaining séances, people saw how quickly she became exhausted, and afterwards they stayed away. Some were afraid she might die while possessed. Others considered themselves partly responsible for what was happening to her and she did nothing to discourage their beliefs.

And then everything changed.

3

Everything began with Jesus on his cross. More specifically, the *shadow* of Jesus on his cross, but Jesus on his cross all the same.

The shell of the church was completed in April, and

immediately the ornate front doors were in place there was a ceremony at which the cross and bleeding wooden figure were nailed together and raised. The nailing was done by a succession of what she supposed were Catholic priests gathered from the other Catholic churches in the district. She watched them over her dangerous lavenders from her upstairs room. The gathered crowd applauded each hammer-blow, and the priests posed for photographs, each with his hammer held aloft. The cross with its burden was then manhandled into position and held in place by ropes and a wooden frame until its concrete foundations set hard. Jesus looked down at the crowd. There was blood on his forehead and face from the crown of thorns, and blood running down his side from the wound of a solitary short arrow. There was no sign of blood where the nails had punctured his palms and feet.

Everything changed when Jesus spoke to her.

She'd gone out when the crowd had dispersed and looked up at him inside his mesh of wood and rope. He'd been beautifully chiselled and painted. The hollow curve of his stomach fell smoothly into his loincloth and rose in obvious pain into his protruding ribcage. He looked down at her and she saw the mirror of her own pity reflected in his eyes.

You've suffered, she said to him, meaning the priests with their hammers, the crowd jostling for photographs, and the crude construction in which he was still held. She was not a religious woman, but the perfectly sculpted body stretched in unendurable pain appealed to her.

The voice told her she was right.

She was panting, still trying to catch her breath from crossing the road, and not looking directly at him when he spoke.

His eyes were open and mournful. He was alive but

dying, would forever be alive but dying. The ground beneath him was strewn with rubble but would soon be seeded with a lawn. It was growing dark, but when the church was eventually opened for services there would be a spotlight casting his formless shadow up into each night.

Her first feeling was to distrust what she'd heard. She looked around her.

You've suffered, she repeated, testing him.

The voice said that suffering was never enough. Being seen to suffer was important, but that too was never enough. Something more was required.

What? she asked, beginning to feel foolish, and again looking around her, this time to see if anyone had heard her.

There was no answer; the mournful eyes continued to stare down at her and she shared in their suffering. She would suffer herself when she re-crossed the road and when she climbed the stairs to bed.

What? she asked again, more loudly. But the voice remained silent.

She left Jesus on his cross and returned home.

The following day she phoned the council and agreed to have her lavender bushes felled. The man on the phone told her there was no longer any real urgency. She told him that one of the bushes had swayed in the wind and she was certain that it threatened to fall. She told him she'd had a dream in which it had fallen and killed a schoolgirl, and being what she was –

Three days later, two men arrived, spent an hour and felled her bushes. Her view of the street beyond was immediately widened in scope. To extend it further she arranged for someone else to come and remove several more of the smaller bushes. The work continued until Jesus on his cross stood revealed to her in his entirety.

Before the opening of the church to its worshippers,

the crucified figure was hosed down and cleaned by two men with brushes.

In June the evening shadow reached across the road and into her garden. She studied it on the longest day to see exactly how close it came to her and marked the point with a wooden stake.

She went back to stand beneath him and he spoke to her for a second time. She asked him if he spoke to everyone and heard his gentle laughter. His expression changed with the fading light and he flinched and fell silent in the headlights of passing cars.

What you do . . . he said to her.

What I do?

How you live . . .

How I –?

He would surely see how nervous she was by the way she wrung her hands.

She wanted to explain to him. Her last séance had been almost six weeks ago, the one before that a month earlier, and both had been half-hearted affairs. Several clients had enquired about further sittings but she'd made excuses and put them off.

How you live, the voice repeated.

She'd known from the very first day how she lived. A small part – a very small part – of her became indignant and almost demanded to know what he was insinuating. An even smaller part of her would have responded to any further criticism by pointing out that he lived in exactly the same way.

But he's always dying, she thought. He was born and lived only to die. She, on the other hand –

The conviction that she was no longer dying left her and she struggled to regain it.

The voice interrupted her thoughts. It continued monosyllabically in the same low tone.

I don't blame, it said. I know, but I don't blame.

What I do, she said – people need to believe. Like they need to believe in you, she wanted to add.

Jesus only smiled. And look what happened to me, the smile told her. She looked. There was already dirt and cobwebs in the creases of his loincloth, between his toes, in his hair, over his legs.

She wondered if she was prepared or equipped for the direction the discussion might now take. If that was what it was. When she wanted him to answer there was only silence; and when she least expected it, he spoke.

She went out to him most evenings during the rest of the summer, but nine nights out of ten she left him disappointed, having heard and achieved nothing. She looked out at him in the growing darkness from her upstairs room.

She held a final, private séance for a woman who had recently lost her husband and was desperate to contact him. She knew nothing about the woman or her husband and so the sitting was a difficult one. She wanted to be told about the man before she gave anything in return. But the woman, having expected so much, and having wanted to believe in her abilities, became sceptical. When her husband finally arrived from the spirit world his passage was a difficult one. She wanted to know if he was still in any pain. No, no pain. The woman became suspicious, withdrew her hands and held them together. She lit a cigarette and then refused to extinguish it. The spirits were repelled by smoke. Surprising, the woman said, considering that her husband had smoked fifty a day. The woman asked her more awkward questions. What could she do? She offered a refund. The woman threatened to expose her; her husband had been an important and influential man. Then why are you here? she thought. The woman's answers were prepared and unassailable. She wanted to tell her about Jesus on his cross, but didn't, and was relieved when she finally went. She kept the woman's money but refused to spend it.

There had been a moment, when the woman had threatened to denounce her, when she'd experienced a fleeting, almost exciting sense of relief.

That night she went back out to Jesus.

She stood beneath him and asked him what he wanted her to do. Jesus didn't speak.

Speak to me, she wanted to shout up at him. His feet were low enough for her to touch, resting now on a board announcing the times of the services in the new church, giving small relief to his suffering.

I know what I've done, she wanted to say. But you spoke to me – *you*. It must count for something.

No answer. She waited.

The houses on either side of her had started to empty as her neighbours sold up and moved on ahead of the bulldozers.

What you do is perfect, the voice said unexpectedly.

It wasn't what she wanted to hear. She wondered if she'd misheard.

Perfect?

Perfect. This, too, is perfect, the voice said. His eyes glanced up to his forehead down to his hands, his side, his feet.

How can it be perfect?

How can it be otherwise?

But she'd never heard a voice in her life before. What if all this had happened forty years ago?

Perfect, the voice repeated, and she knew from its tone that the conversation was over.

She left him, unsatisfied and disillusioned, and returned home.

Making her breakfast the following morning she dropped the kettle and scalded her leg. She treated herself, and only when the blistered skin became septic did she call the doctor, who sent for an ambulance to take her to the hospital, where she had her leg treated properly, stayed for the afternoon and was then brought home.

She couldn't walk across to Jesus, but she told him about her leg from the upstairs room.

When she had fully recovered – in so far as she fully recovered from anything at her age – she went back out to him. But he remained silent into the winter months. She told him about the war and how she'd started, about Brighton, her return to London, the business she'd built up. She tapped the wood of his upright as though this might elicit some response. After the third unsuccessful month she stopped trying.

Jesus never spoke to her again, and she never knew if he'd been applauding or condemning what she did.

Old clients still occasionally called, but she told them it was all over, never to be repeated. Some assumed she'd lost the gift; others said they knew all along that she'd never had it. Believe what you like, she thought, you still came, you still came back for more, and would have come back again if I'd offered.

Why had it mattered?

What difference would it have made if Jesus had never spoken to her?

She watched the worshippers filing past his feet and the priests standing in the doorway behind them.

The demolition work approached her and she finally agreed to sell.

Two months before she was due to leave she fell down the stairs and broke her ankle. She remained undiscovered for almost three days. When found, she was unconscious but still alive. She was taken back to the same hospital, this time for a fortnight. There were no visitors, and when the other patients asked her about herself she lied to them.

She returned home in time to supervise the removal of her belongings. She left the table and chairs with which she'd conducted her séances and they were crushed beneath the falling rubble.

Later, she stood with the crowd at a safe distance and watched the heavy lead ball swing into her walls and windows, play first with her chimney stack and then violate the bull's-eye of her door.

Throughout the demolition work Jesus and his cross had been covered and protected by a tarpaulin.

That's right – don't look, she thought. You never saw anything in the past, why should you see anything now? The top of the cross and his outstretched arms were visible only in outline.

We're all frauds one way or another, she thought. Her breathing had deteriorated since her stay in the hospital and walking any distance over fifty yards now caused her great pain. She'd been given an aluminium walking frame but had insisted on using a stick instead.

She believed once again that she was shortly going to die, but this time it was more than a belief. Belief had been what people who had come to see her had had; belief was what she'd had standing beneath Jesus for the first time; belief had been nine tenths of the fraud all along.

She left the crowd and heard people cheering as the last of the masonry crumpled and fell. Everything was behind her. She walked away. If Jesus *had* wanted to speak to her his words would have been muffled by the tarpaulin. Enough was enough.

From her home she moved into a residential centre.

She wanted to help the others, but knew it was beyond her now even to offer.

She died six months later in her sleep, and the few people whose duty it was to care, assured everyone else that she was now in heaven. They said she'd led a good life and that her place in heaven had been guaranteed.

During the hour beforehand she'd been fully awake. She'd asked questions, but, like the ones she'd asked of Jesus, they had remained unanswered. The room around her was filled with stirrings, coughs, and the small, involuntary cries of dreaming sleep. It's like being in a forest in the middle of the night, she thought. Simply being there was a kind of dying. She cleared her mind and it remained empty. She'd been kept off her feet for the previous week and was being given medication to ease her breathing. She was also taking tablets to help her sleep, except that for the last fortnight she'd only pretended to swallow them and had surreptitiously collected them.

Death and heaven were not uncommon to the room in which she slept, and there was little now to choose between living and dying in it. Life itself had become part of a great, undeniable fraud.

The tablets were small, and smooth from where she'd tucked them into her mouth between her gums and lips. There was someone sitting at the far end of the room, writing, surrounded by papers, lit by a dim lamp.

Life, she realised with a sense of relief, had no conclusions to offer her; it was why she had long ago rejected it in favour of the more profitable prospect of death and all *its* uncertainties.

The woman sitting writing by the dim light of the lamp was the last thing she saw.

When the time came, she did not expect Jesus to return to her and lead her by the hand, and when she died she died alone, secure in the peace of what she considered to be a full and almost perfect understanding.

THE ECLIPSE

Augusto Monterroso

Translated from the Spanish by
Norman Thomas di Giovanni and Susan Ashe

When Friar Bartolomé Arrazola saw that he had lost his way he resigned himself to the fact that nothing could save him. He had been swallowed up, irrevocably and forever, by the relentless Guatemalan forest. Utterly unfamiliar with the terrain, he sat down calmly to await death. He wanted to die there, alone, bereft of all hope, his thoughts fixed on faraway Spain and especially on the monastery of Los Abrojos, where once Charles V had deigned to descend from his eminence and tell Bartolomé of his faith in the zeal of the friar's efforts to save souls.

When he awoke he found himself surrounded by a group of inscrutable Indians, who were preparing him on an altar – an altar that seemed to Bartolomé to be the bed on which he was at last to find rest from his fears, from life, from himself.

Three years in that country had given him a fair command of the native tongues. Trying out a few words, he found they were understood.

Then there came to him an idea that arose out of his intellect, his universal learning, and his painstaking study of Aristotle. That very day, he remembered, there was going to be a total eclipse of the sun. In the depth of his being, he resolved to take advantage of this knowledge to fool his captors and save his skin.

'If you kill me,' he told them, 'I will make the sun grow dark in the sky.'

The Indians stared at him, and Bartolomé caught the disbelief in their eyes. He watched while they called a small council and he waited confidently, not without a trace of scorn.

Two hours later, Friar Bartolomé Arrazola's heart spurted violent blood onto the sacrificial stone that gleamed beneath the opaque light of a solar eclipse, while an Indian intoned in succession the endless cycle of dates on which – according to the calculations of Mayan astronomers as written down in their codices without the invaluable help of Aristotle – eclipses of the sun and moon would fall.

BIOGRAPHICAL NOTES

FRANCIS KING was born in Switzerland in 1923 and spent his childhood in India. His years in the British Council took him to Italy, Greece, Egypt, Finland and Japan. In 1963 he resigned to devote himself entirely to writing. His most recently published works are *Frozen Music* (1987), a novella and *The Woman Who Was God* (1988), a novel. He is International President of PEN.

MARCOS AGUINIS, who was born in Cordoba, Argentina, in 1935, was trained as a neurosurgeon and psychoanalyst. He is the author of, among other books, five novels and two story collections. A polemical study of the military mind was published in 1983. He has also been his country's Secretary of Culture and at present is presidential adviser on cultural affairs.

DAVID LEAVITT was born in 1961, grew up in California and graduated from Yale. His first book, a collection of stories entitled *Family Dancing* (1985), was finalist for both the National Book Critics Award and PEN/Faulkner Prize. His first novel, *The Lost Language of Cranes*, was published in 1987 and his new novel, *Gone Tomorrow*, will be published in 1989. He lives in East Hampton, New York.

JEANETTE WINTERSON was born in Lancashire in 1959. Before she read English at Oxford she was a Pentecostal Evangelist. Since then she has dogsbodied in the theatre and worked as a writer full-time. *Oranges Are Not The Only Fruit* won the 1985 Whitbread First Novel Award. *The Passion* won the 1987 John Llewellyn Rhys Memorial Prize. She lives in London.

BIOGRAPHICAL NOTES

DAMON GALGUT was born in 1963 in Pretoria. 1982 saw the publication of his first novel, the highly acclaimed *A Sinless Season* (Penguin). A second book, a collection, *Small circle of beings*, was brought out by Constable this summer. In addition, he is the author of three full-length plays: *Echoes of Anger, Alive and Kicking*, and *A Party for Mother*. He lives in Cape Town.

LAWRENCE SCOTT is from Trinidad and Tobago, now resident in Britain. He has had short stories published in the *Trinidad and Tobago Review, Chelsea* and *The PEN*. He was awarded the 1986 Tom-Gallon Award for his short story 'The house of funerals'. He teaches English at the Islington Sixth Form Centre (ILEA) and divides his time between teaching and writing. He is now completing his first novel and has a collection of stories prepared for publication.

MONICA FURLONG is a biographer and novelist. Her biographies include *Merton* (1980), *Genuine Fake* (1986), and *Therese of Lisieux* (1987, for Virago). Her novels are *The Cat's Eye* (1976), *Cousins* (1983) and *Wise Child* (1987, now being made into a film).

PETER BENSON was born in England in 1956 and was educated in Ramsgate, Canterbury and Exeter. He worked at a variety of jobs before his first novel *The Levels* was published in 1987. It won a Betty Trask Award, Guardian Fiction Prize, the Authors' Club First Novel Award, and was short-listed for the Whitbread Prize (First Novel) and the David Higham Prize. This is the second year he has contributed to *Winter's Tales*.

SUE KRISMAN grew up in Portsmouth and now lives

in Berkshire with her husband and teenage children. After some years as Writer in Residence at Bulmershe College of Higher Education, where her third novel *So Long as They're Cheering* (1986) was researched and written, she became Creative Writing Fellow at the University of Reading, and is now writing full time. Her other works include two novels, *The Thursby People* (1979) and *Ducks and Drakes* (1981) and an original opera libretto.

DESMOND HOGAN is aged 37, from County Galway. In 1987 his selected early stories *The Mourning Thief and other stories* were published by Faber and Faber. His most recent novels are: *A Curious Street* (1984, Picador) and *A New Shirt* (1986, Faber paperbacks). His most recent book is a collection of stories *Lebanon Lodge and other stories* (1988, Faber and Faber). In 1988 he was one of the three non-American writers invited to take part in the World Writers' Series at the Central University of Florida.

LAURA KALPAKIAN is the author of many short stories published on both sides of the Atlantic, as well as three previous novels: *Beggars and Choosers* (1978, USA only), *These Latter days* (1985) and *The Swallow Inheritance* (1987) both available in softcover from Headline. A native Californian she currently teaches at Western Washington University, Bellingham, USA.

HELEN HARRIS is the author of two novels: *Playing Fields in Winter* (1986) and *Angel Cake* (1987) (both Century Hutchinson). She has published some twenty-five short stories in a wide variety of magazines and anthologies ranging from *Encounter* and *London Magazine* to *Punch* and *Penguin Firebird Collection*. She has lived in London for the past ten years, but travels very widely, recently visiting the Middle East, India and the Far East.

ROBERT EDRIC was born in Sheffield in 1956. He has published two novels *Winter Garden* (1985) winner of the James Tait Black Memorial Award, and *A New Ice Age* (1986) runner-up for the Guardian Fiction Prize, and his short stories have appeared in *The London Magazine, Stand, Critical Quarterly* and *PEN New Fiction*. A new novel, *A Lunar Eclipse* is to be published in spring 1989.

AUGUSTO MONTERROSO is a Guatemalan, who has lived in political exile in Mexico for some thirty years. He is the author of several collections of elegant and funny short stories and essays that often blur the line between the two forms. Mild-mannered and in his mid-sixties, he nonetheless represents a threat to the US government, which will not allow him to visit the country.